First World War
and Army of Occupation
War Diary
France, Belgium and Germany

28 DIVISION
83 Infantry Brigade
King's Own (Royal Lancaster Regiment)
2nd Battalion
22 December 1914 - 31 October 1915

WO95/2274/2

The Naval & Military Press Ltd
www.nmarchive.com
Published in association with The National Archives

Published by

The Naval & Military Press Ltd

Unit 10 Ridgewood Industrial Park,

Uckfield, East Sussex,

TN22 5QE England

Tel: +44 (0) 1825 749494

www.naval-military-press.com

www.nmarchive.com

This diary has been reprinted in facsimile from the original. Any imperfections are inevitably reproduced and the quality may fall short of modern type and cartographic standards.

Contents

Document type	Place/Title	Date From	Date To
Heading	WO95/2274/2		
Heading	28th Division 83rd Infy Bde 2nd Bn King's Own R.L.R. Dec 1914-Oct 1915 To Salonika		
Heading	83rd Bde. 28th Div. War Diary 2nd K.O.R. Lancs. 22nd December 1914 To 1st March 1915 Oct 15		
War Diary	Plymouth	22/12/1914	24/12/1914
War Diary	Winchester	24/12/1914	14/01/1915
War Diary	Hursley Park	01/01/1915	01/01/1915
War Diary	Fawley Down	12/01/1915	15/01/1915
War Diary	Havre	16/01/1915	18/01/1915
War Diary	Hazebrook	18/01/1915	08/02/1915
War Diary	Ouderdom	09/02/1915	20/02/1915
War Diary	Blauw Port Farm	20/02/1915	21/02/1915
War Diary	Ypres	21/02/1915	21/02/1915
War Diary	Ouderdom	21/02/1915	01/03/1915
Heading	83rd Bde. 28th Div. War Diary 2nd K.O.R. Lancs. March 1915		
Heading	War Diary Of 2nd Bn The King's Own Regt. From 1/3/15 To 31/3/15		
War Diary		01/03/1915	01/03/1915
War Diary	Ouderdom	02/03/1915	03/03/1915
War Diary	Bailleul	03/03/1915	11/03/1915
War Diary	Dranoutre	12/03/1915	31/03/1915
Heading	83rd Bde. 28th Div. War Diary 2nd K.O.R. Lancs. April 1915		
Heading	28th Division 2nd Royal Lancs Vol III 1.4-3.5.15		
Heading	War Diary Of 2nd Bn The King's Own Regt From 1.4.15 To 3.5.15		
War Diary	Neuve Eglise	01/04/1915	08/04/1915
War Diary	Boeschepe	06/04/1915	08/04/1915
War Diary	Ypres	09/04/1915	20/04/1915
War Diary	Zonnebeke	20/04/1915	03/05/1915
Heading	83rd Bde. 28th Div. 2nd King's Own Royal Lancs May 1915 Report On Enemy Attack Of Frezenberg Trenches 8.5.15		
Heading	War Diary Of 2nd Bn The King's Own Regt. From 4.5.15 To 28.5.15 Volume 4		
War Diary	Huts W Of Ypres	04/05/1915	08/05/1915
War Diary	Frezenburg	08/05/1915	09/05/1915
War Diary	Huts W Of Ypres	10/05/1915	28/05/1915
Heading	Reports Attack Frezenberg On Enemy 8.5.15		
Miscellaneous	Headquarters 3rd Brigade	11/05/1915	11/05/1915
Miscellaneous	Hd. Qrs 83rd Bde	07/05/1915	07/05/1915
Diagram etc	20 Innovation Officer 62nd Battery R.F.A.		
Miscellaneous	C Form (Original) Messages And Signals		
Miscellaneous	A Form. Messages And Signals		
Miscellaneous	A Form. Messages And Signals	05/05/1915	05/05/1915
Heading	83rd Bde. 28th Division. War Diary 2nd King's Own Royal Lancs June 1915		
War Diary		01/06/1915	30/06/1915

Heading	83rd Bde. 28th Div. War Diary 2nd King's Own Royal Lancs. July 1915		
Heading	War Diary Of 2nd Bn. The King's Own Regiment From 1.7.15 To 31.7.15 Vol 6		
War Diary		01/07/1915	31/07/1915
Heading	83rd Bde. 28th Division. War Diary 2nd King's Own Royal Lancs. August 1915		
Heading	War Diary Of 2nd Bn The King's Own Regt. From 1.8.15 To 31.8.1915 Volume 7		
War Diary	Wolvergom	01/08/1915	05/08/1915
War Diary	Scherpenberg	06/08/1915	11/08/1915
War Diary	Kemmel	12/08/1915	17/08/1915
War Diary	Scherpenberg	18/08/1915	23/08/1915
War Diary	Kemmel	24/08/1915	29/08/1915
War Diary	Scherpenberg	30/08/1915	31/08/1915
Operation(al) Order(s)	Operation Orders No. 24 By Lieut. Colonel E.M. Morris, Commdg. 2nd. Bn. The King's Own Regiment App I	29/07/1915	29/07/1915
Operation(al) Order(s)	Operation Order No. 11 By Brig. General G.E. Pereira Commanding 85th Inf. Brigade. App 2	01/08/1915	01/08/1915
Operation(al) Order(s)	Operation Order No. 26 By Lieut. Colonel E.M. Morris, Commdg. 2nd. Bn. The King's Own Regiment App 3	11/08/1915	11/08/1915
Operation(al) Order(s)	Operation Order No. 59 By Brigadier General H.S.L. Ravenshaw C.M.G. Commanding 83rd Infantry Brigade App 3	10/08/1915	10/08/1915
Operation(al) Order(s)	Operation Order No. 61 By Brigadier-General H.S.L. Ravenshaw, C.M.G. Commanding 83rd Infantry Brigade App 4	12/08/1915	12/08/1915
Operation(al) Order(s)	Operation Order No. 62 by Brigadier General H.S.L. Ravenshaw C.M.G. Commanding 83rd Infantry Brigade App 5	16/08/1915	16/08/1915
Operation(al) Order(s)	Operation Orders No. 28 By Lieut. Col. E.M. Morris Commd Bn. The King Own Regt App 5	17/08/1915	17/08/1915
Operation(al) Order(s)	Operation Order No. 65 By Brigadier General H.S.L. Ravenshaw C.M.G. Commanding 83rd Infantry Brigade App 6	22/08/1915	22/08/1915
Operation(al) Order(s)	Operation Orders No. 29 By Lieut. Colonel E.M. Morris, Commdg. 2nd. Bn. The King's Own Regiment App 6	23/08/1915	23/08/1915
Operation(al) Order(s)	Operation Order No. 66 By Brigadier General H.S.L. Ravenshaw C.M.G. Commanding 83rd Infantry Brigade App 7	27/08/1915	27/08/1915
Operation(al) Order(s)	Operation Orders No. 30 By Lieut. Col. E.M. Morris Commdg Bn The King's Own Regt App 7	29/08/1915	29/08/1915
Heading	83rd Bde. 28th Division War Diary 2nd King's Own Royal Lancs September 1915		
War Diary	Scherpenberg	01/09/1915	04/09/1915
War Diary	Kemmel	05/09/1915	10/09/1915
War Diary	Locre	11/09/1915	16/09/1915
War Diary	Kemmel	17/09/1915	22/09/1915
War Diary	Clap Bank	23/09/1915	26/09/1915
War Diary	Robecq	27/09/1915	27/09/1915
War Diary	Noyelles	28/09/1915	29/09/1915
War Diary	Quarry Trench	30/09/1915	30/09/1915

Heading	83rd Bde. 28th Div. War Diary Embarked With Division For Salonika 1.11.15. 2nd K.O.R. Lancs October 1915		
War Diary		01/10/1915	01/10/1915
War Diary	Annequin	02/10/1915	03/10/1915
War Diary	Big Willie	03/10/1915	06/10/1915
War Diary	Annequin	06/10/1915	06/10/1915
War Diary	Gonnehem	07/10/1915	15/10/1915
War Diary	La Preol	16/10/1915	16/10/1915
War Diary	Cuinchy	18/10/1915	21/10/1915
War Diary	Gonnehem	21/10/1915	22/10/1915
War Diary	Marseilles	25/10/1915	25/10/1915
War Diary	S.S. Alnwick Castle	26/10/1915	31/10/1915
Miscellaneous	A Form. Messages And Signals		
Heading	C Form (Quadruplicate). Messages And Signals	03/10/1915	03/10/1915
Miscellaneous	A Form Messages And Signals		
Miscellaneous	Messages And Signals		
Miscellaneous	C Form (Duplicate) Messages And Signals	04/10/1915	04/10/1915
Miscellaneous	A Form Messages And Signals		
Miscellaneous	Messages And Signals		
Miscellaneous	A Form Messages And Signals		
Miscellaneous	Messages And Signals		
Miscellaneous	A Form Messages And Signals		

28TH DIVISION
83RD INFY BDE

2ND BN KING'S OWN R.L.R.
DEC 1914-OCT 1915

TO SALONIKA

83rd Bde.
28th Div.

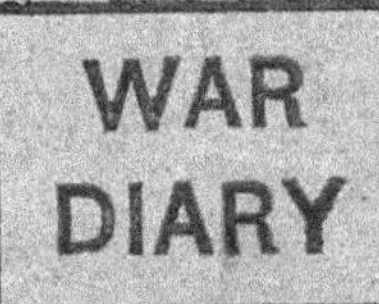

2nd K. O. R. LANCS.

22ND DECEMBER 1914

TO

1ST MARCH

1 9 1 5

Army Form C. 2118.

Instructions regarding War Diaries and Intelligence Summaries are contained in F. S. Regs., Part II. and the Staff Manual respectively. Title pages will be prepared in manuscript.

WAR DIARY
or
INTELLIGENCE SUMMARY
(Erase heading not required.)

Hour, Date, Place	Summary of Events and Information	Remarks and references to Appendices
4 P.M. 22nd Dec. 1914 PLYMOUTH	Arrived from INDIA by S.S. KENILWORTH CASTLE and began to disembark	
6.30 A.M. 7 A.M. 23rd Dec. "	Entrained for WINCHESTER and on arrival marched to HURSLEY PARK Camp, arriving 5 P.M.	
24th Dec. – 14th Jan. 1915 WINCHESTER	Mobilising	
4.30 P.M. Jan. 1st HURSLEY PARK	Marched into billets at WINCHESTER COLLEGE	
10.30 A.M. Jan. 12th FAWLEY DOWN	Attended Divisional Parade for Inspection by H.M. the King	
8.15 A.M. Jan. 15th	Marched from WINCHESTER to SOUTHAMPTON and embarked there at 1.30 P.M. sailing 5.30 P.M. in S.S. NOVIAN to HAVRE.	

1247 W 3299 200,000 (E) 8/14 J.B.C. & A. Forms/C. 2118/11.

2

Instructions regarding War Diaries and Intelligence Summaries are contained in F. S. Regs., Part II. and the Staff Manual respectively. Title pages will be prepared in manuscript.

WAR DIARY
or
INTELLIGENCE SUMMARY
(Erase heading not required.)

Army Form C. 2118.

Hour, Date, Place	Summary of Events and Information	Remarks and references to Appendices
10 A.M. Jan. 16th HAVRE	Began to disembark and at 6.30 P.M. marched to rest camp at GRANVILLE.	
1. P.M. Jan. 17th "	Marched from GRANVILLE Camp to Station	
5.30. P.M.	and entrained, leaving for HAZEBROOK 5.30 P.M.	
4.15. P.M. Jan 18th HAZEBROOK	Arrived HAZEBROOK and billeted there for night	
9. A.M. Jan. 19th "	Marched to billets at CLAPBANK 1 mile S.W. of BAILLEUL and remained there till Feb 1st	
1. P.M. Feb. 1st	Left CLAPBANK by motor bus for VLAMERTINGHE and and bivouaced there	
12.15. A.M. & 4 A.M. Feb. 2nd	Marched by half Battalions at 12.15 A.M. and 4 A.M. to YITVERHOEK and YPRES	
3. P.M. Feb. 3rd	Marched to YPRES and at 5.30 A.M. marched to Bde. H.Qs. S. of YPRES and thence to trenches S. of Canal near OOSTHOEK.	
Feb. 4th	In trenches	

1247 W 3299 200,000 (E) 8/14 J.B.C. & A. Forms/C. 2118/11.

3/

Instructions regarding War Diaries and Intelligence Summaries are contained in F. S. Regs., Part II. and the Staff Manual respectively. Title pages will be prepared in manuscript.

WAR DIARY
or
INTELLIGENCE SUMMARY

(Erase heading not required.)

Army Form C. 2118.

Hour, Date, Place	Summary of Events and Information	Remarks and references to Appendices
Feb. 5th	In trenches	
8.P.M. Feb. 6th to 4.A.M. Feb. 7th	Were relieved in trenches by 3rd Middlesex Regt. and moved into billets in Cavalry Barracks YPRES. During this tour of duty in the trenches the Battalion lost Officers nil, Other Ranks 7 killed and 46 wounded, and at the termination of the tour one Officer (Lieut. V. L. de Cordova) and about 140 N.C.O.s & men were sent to hospital suffering from [what is described by the Medical authorities as] frost-bite. All ranks had had feet and legs from just above the knee rubbed with whale oil before proceeding to the trenches. Some of the trenches were bad from the point of view of wet and mud and especially the trench in which Lieut. de Cordova had been.	
12 Noon Feb. 7th	Marched between 12 noon and 1 P.M. by Coys. to OUDERDOM	
Feb. 8th	Rested at OUDERDOM	

4

WAR DIARY
or
INTELLIGENCE SUMMARY
(Erase heading not required.)

Instructions regarding War Diaries and Intelligence Summaries are contained in F. S. Regs., Part II. and the Staff Manual respectively. Title pages will be prepared in manuscript.

Army Form C. 2118.

Hour, Date, Place	Summary of Events and Information	Remarks and references to Appendices
Feb. 9th OUDERDOM	Rested, drawing up requirements.	
12 Noon Feb. 10th	Moved into billets just S. of OUDERDOM	
3.30. P.M. Feb. 11th	Marched to YPRES	
6.30. P.M. Feb. 11th	H.Qs. B and D Companies marched from YPRES to the TUILLERIES just N. of ZILLEBEKE where they remained in support of the E. YORKSHIRE Regt. who held the trenches in the left Section of the line held by the Brigade. A and C Companies remained in YPRES.	
Feb. 12th	Remained in Support	
8 P.M. Feb. 13th	Relieved the E. YORKS Regt. in the Trenches. H.Qs at ZILLEBEKE FARM.	
8. P.M. Feb. 15th	The Battalion was relieved in the fire trenches by the E. YORKS Regt. and was disposed as follows.	

1247 W 3299 200,000 (E) 8/14 J.B.C. & A. Forms/C. 2118/11.

6

Instructions regarding War Diaries and Intelligence Summaries are contained in F. S. Regs., Part II. and the Staff Manual respectively. Title pages will be prepared in manuscript.

WAR DIARY
or
INTELLIGENCE SUMMARY
(Erase heading not required.)

Army Form C. 2118.

2/4th

Hour, Date, Place	Summary of Events and Information	Remarks and references to Appendices
10.15 A.M. Feb. 14th	B, D and ½ C Coy moved up by orders from the Brigade and remained with A Coy working in the trenches throughout the day, and took over part of the fire trenches in the night. The German attack and our counter-attack had taken place round part of the ruined hamlet of ZWARTELEN. In the assault made by A Coy. and in the subsequent operations of the day the Battalion lost 4 [the following] Officers	
	Killed 4: Lieut. H. D. STOKES M.V.O.; " G. L. HARFORD killed while leading the charge; 2nd " D. YORKE; " " T. H. HATHAWAY	
	Wounded 1: Major O. C. BORRETT	
	and of other ranks	
	Killed 18	
	Wounded 33	

1247 W 3299 200,000 (E) 8/14 J.B.C. & A. Forms/C. 2118/11.

5

Instructions regarding War Diaries and Intelligence Summaries are contained in F. S. Regs., Part II. and the Staff Manual respectively. Title pages will be prepared in manuscript.

WAR DIARY
or
INTELLIGENCE SUMMARY
(Erase heading not required.)

Army Form C. 2118.

Hour, Date, Place	Summary of Events and Information	Remarks and references to Appendices
	B, D & ½ C Coys. at the TUILLERIES, A Coy in close support of the Fire Trenches in a support trench (A_2) and "dug outs" U on the right of the left section & ½ C in "dug outs" on the left of the left section in close support.	
Feb. 16th	Remained as above.	
6.30. A.M. Feb. 17th	The Company in close support on the right at Trench A_2 and "Dug-outs" at U was called upon to re-inforce the E. YORKS Regt. one of whose trenches B_2 had been taken by the enemy.	
10. A.M. Feb. 17th	The Enemy were assaulted with the bayonet by "A" Coy. under command of Major O.C. BORRETT and the lost trench re-taken.	

4

Instructions regarding War Diaries and Intelligence Summaries are contained in F. S. Regs., Part II. and the Staff Manual respectively. Title pages will be prepared in manuscript.

WAR DIARY
or
INTELLIGENCE SUMMARY
(Erase heading not required.)

Army Form C. 2118.

Hour, Date, Place	Summary of Events and Information	Remarks and references to Appendices
Feb. 18th & 19th	The Battalion remained in the Fire Trenches including ½ "C" Coy from the "dug outs" on the left, who were moved into the fire trenches.	
10 P.M. Feb. 19th – 4 A.M. " 20th	The Battalion was relieved partly by E. YORKS Regt and partly by K.O.Y.L.I. with the exception of "B" who remained in the trenches.	
	The remainder of the Battalion moved as follows H. Qrs. A, D, & ½ C Coys. to BLAUWPORT FARM in the Right Section of the Brigade line, in Support; ½ C Coy. to "dug outs" behind the right fire trenches The relief was not completed until 4 A.M. on the 20th	
2.30. P.M. Feb. 20th BLAUWPORT FARM	Request received from O.C. Right Section to hold one Company in readiness. "B" Coy was detailed and in	

1247 W 3299 200,000 (E) 8/14 J.B.C. & A. Forms/C. 2118/11.

8

Instructions regarding War Diaries and Intelligence Summaries are contained in F. S. Regs., Part II. and the Staff Manual respectively. Title pages will be prepared in manuscript.

WAR DIARY
or
INTELLIGENCE SUMMARY
(Erase heading not required.)

Army Form C. 2118.

Hour, Date, Place	Summary of Events and Information	Remarks and references to Appendices
3.15 P.M. Feb. 20th	response to a message from O.C. Right Section desiring them to move up in support, left BLAUWPORT FARM at 3.15 P.M. with instructions to report to O.C. Right Section. The Company together with the ½ of "C" Coy. in the "Dug outs" was apparently placed under orders of the G.O.C. 84th Brigade and employed in an attack intended to re-take a trench, which had been taken by the Enemy from that Brigade.	FEW
8. P.M. Feb. 20th	A N.C.O. arrived at BLAUWPORT FARM and reported that all the Officers of the Company and a half had been shot down, that a few of the rank & file had reached & entered the trench which was the object of attack and found it empty except for dead Germans and had been led out of the trench by an Officer of another regiment.	FEW

9

Instructions regarding War Diaries and Intelligence Summaries are contained in F. S. Regs., Part II. and the Staff Manual respectively. Title pages will be prepared in manuscript.

WAR DIARY
or
INTELLIGENCE SUMMARY
(Erase heading not required.)

Army Form C. 2118.

Hour, Date, Place	Summary of Events and Information	Remarks and references to Appendices
9 P.M. Feb. 20th	The Battalion was relieved at BLAUWPORT FARM by the 2nd Btn. K.O.Y.L.I., a unit of the relieving 13th Bde, and marched to YPRES. The remains of the Company and a Half which had been sent to assist the 84th Bde (D & ½ "C" Coys) also returned to YPRES, and so too the Company "B" which had been left in the fire trenches of the Left Section. In the attack under orders of the G.O.C. 84th Bde. in which D and ½ C Coys. took part the Battalion suffered the following losses Killed Officers nil (as far as ascertained) Other Ranks 6 Wounded Officers 2 [Capt. H.A. KAULBACH / " R.A. RAY] Other Ranks 42	

1247 W 3299 200,000 (E) 8/14 J.B.C. & A. Forms/C. 2118/11.

10

Instructions regarding War Diaries and Intelligence Summaries are contained in F. S. Regs., Part II. and the Staff Manual respectively. Title pages will be prepared in manuscript.

WAR DIARY
or
INTELLIGENCE SUMMARY
(Erase heading not required.)

Army Form C. 2118.

Hour, Date, Place	Summary of Events and Information	Remarks and references to Appendices
	Wounded and Missing 2nd Lieut. R. M. F. ROSS	
	Missing Other Ranks 4	
1.30. A.M. Feb 21st YPRES	At YPRES the troops were given hot tea and some food and at 1.30. A.M. on the 21st marched to huts between VLAMERTINGHE and OUDERDOM,	
3.30. A.M. Feb. 21st OUDERDOM	arriving about 3.30. A.M.	
	During this tour in the trenches the Battalion lost Killed Officers 4 Other Ranks 31 Wounded Officers 3 Other Ranks 49 Missing Officers 1 Other Ranks 4 The great majority of these ~~were~~ losses occurred in the attacks of the 14th and 20th	

1247 W 3299 200,000 (E) 8/14 J.B.C. & A. Forms/C. 2118/11.

11

Instructions regarding War Diaries and Intelligence Summaries are contained in F. S. Regs., Part II. and the Staff Manual respectively. Title pages will be prepared in manuscript.

WAR DIARY
or
INTELLIGENCE SUMMARY

(Erase heading not required.)

Army Form C. 2118.

Hour, Date, Place	Summary of Events and Information	Remarks and references to Appendices
	At the conclusion of this tour of duty in the trenches the Battalion also lost a/c feet about 80 N.C.Os & men.	
	Previous to this tour a special anti-frostbite grease had been used instead of the whale oil used in the first tour.	
Feb. 22nd OUDERDOM	Remained in huts at OUDERDOM	
	Hot Baths were arranged for the troops in schools about 2 miles away.	

1247 W 3299 200,000 (E) 8/14 J.B.C. & A. Forms/C. 2118/11.

12

Instructions regarding War Diaries and Intelligence Summaries are contained in F. S. Regs., Part II. and the Staff Manual respectively. Title pages will be prepared in manuscript.

WAR DIARY
or
INTELLIGENCE SUMMARY
(Erase heading not required.)

Army Form C. 2118.

Hour, Date, Place	Summary of Events and Information	Remarks and references to Appendices
Feb. 23rd – 26th OUDERDOM	The Battalion remained in huts about 1 mile N. of OUDERDOM A draft of 50 men under command of 2nd Lieut G.L. SOMMERVILLE which had arrived during the last tour of duty in the trenches was posted to companies.	
5.30 P.M. Feb. 26th	The Battalion marched to YPRES en route to a further tour of duty in the trenches	
8.40 P.M. Feb 26th	The Battalion [after teas in the Drapers Hall] marched to trenches via ZILLEBEKE, B Coy to trench 50, C & D Companies to trench 49, Head Quarters & A Coy to trench 51	
Feb. 24th – March 1st	In trenches. B Coy remained throughout in 50 Trench, A, C & D Companies each passed 2 nights in fire trench 49 & 1 night in support trench 51.	

1247 W 3299 200,000 (E) 8/14 J.B.C. & A. Forms/C. 2118/11.

83rd Bde.
28th Div.

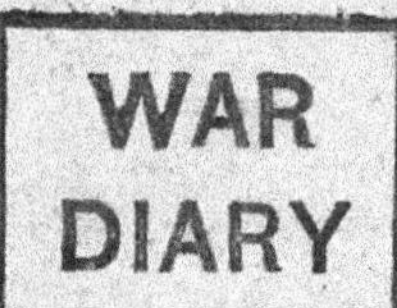

2nd K. O. R. LANCS.

MARCH

1 9 1 5.

Confidential

War Diary

of

2nd Bn The King's Own Regt.

From 1/3/15 To 31/3/15

13

Instructions regarding War Diaries and Intelligence Summaries are contained in F. S. Regs., Part II. and the Staff Manual respectively. Title pages will be prepared in manuscript.

WAR DIARY
or
INTELLIGENCE SUMMARY
(Erase heading not required.)

Army Form C. 2118.

Hour, Date, Place	Summary of Events and Information	Remarks and references to Appendices
9 P.M. March 1st	The Battalion was relieved by Companies by the Duke of Wellington's and R. W. Kent Regts. and marched to YPRES	
3.A.M. March 2nd OUDERDOM	Thence after teas to huts about 1 mile N. of OUDERDOM	
	During their tour in the trenches the Battalion lost	
	Officers nil	
	Other Ranks Killed 2 Wounded 2.	
	The Battalion also lost about another 40 men a/c feet.	
	A draft of 140 N.C.O.s & men which had arrived on Feb. 28th was posted to Companies, bringing up the strength of the Battalion to a total all ranks of 514.	
	Hot Baths were arranged for 100 men.	

14

Instructions regarding War Diaries and Intelligence Summaries are contained in F. S. Regs., Part II. and the Staff Manual respectively. Title pages will be prepared in manuscript.

WAR DIARY
or
INTELLIGENCE SUMMARY
(Erase heading not required.)

Army Form C. 2118.

Hour, Date, Place	Summary of Events and Information	Remarks and references to Appendices
8.A.M. March 3rd	The Battalion marched with remainder of the Brigade by RENINGHELST, WESTOUTRE & CROIX DE POPERINGUE to BAILLEUL and went into billets. The 5th Battalion (Territorial) of the Regiment recently arrived from England & attached to the Brigade turned out to greet the Battalion.	2/A
March 3rd – 4th BAILLEUL	The Battalion remained in billets at BAILLEUL and re-fitted. Baths were arranged for the troops.	
2.15 P.M. March 4th	The Battalion marched to billets in DRANOUTRE preparatory to relieving the 2/ E. YORKSHIRE Regt. in the trenches.	

15

Instructions regarding War Diaries and Intelligence Summaries are contained in F. S. Regs., Part II. and the Staff Manual respectively. Title pages will be prepared in manuscript.

WAR DIARY
or
INTELLIGENCE SUMMARY

(Erase heading not required.)

Army Form C. 2118.

Hour, Date, Place	Summary of Events and Information	Remarks and references to Appendices
March 8th – 10th	Remained in billets in DRANOUTRE	
March 10th	Notification appeared in Bde. Orders of the Grant of Distinguished Conduct Medal to No. 10584 Pte. PARKS who though wounded on the way when sent on a message to the Officer Commanding his Company, delivered the message, took part in the assault at ZWARTALEN and returned with a message before going to Hospital.	
5.P.M. March 11th	The Battalion proceeded to the Trenches to relieve the E. YORSHIRE Regt. & occupied fire trenches known as 14 b and 15 & support trenches 14 b & 15 with supporting companies at COOKER FARM and COB FARM and Battalion H. Qrs. & dressing station at TEA FARM all in Sector E	
	A draft of 100 accompanied by Capt. C. W. Brewer and 2nd Lieuts. Mitchell and Scudamore arrived the same day and remained in DRANOUTRE	

1247 W 3299 200,000 (E) 8/14 J.B.C. & A. Forms/C. 2118/11.

16

Instructions regarding War Diaries and Intelligence Summaries are contained in F. S. Regs., Part II. and the Staff Manual respectively. Title pages will be prepared in manuscript.

WAR DIARY
or
INTELLIGENCE SUMMARY
(Erase heading not required.)

Army Form C. 2118.

Hour, Date, Place	Summary of Events and Information	Remarks and references to Appendices
March 12th – 17th	The Battalion remained in Trenches etc.	[illegible]
March 13th DRANOUTRE	A draft of 12 (7 of whom were men discharged from Hospital) arrived in DRANOUTRE	[illegible]
March 15th DRANOUTRE	A draft of 111 accompanied by 2nd Lieuts. HORNE and TAYLOR arrived in DRANOUTRE	[illegible]
March 17th – 18th	On the night of March 17/18 the Battalion was relieved by the 2/ E. YORKSHIRE Regt. and returned to previous billets in DRANOUTRE.	[illegible]
	During this tour in the trenches the Battalion lost no Officers, but of other ranks 8 killed and 12 wounded. The majority of these losses occurred on the day of the unsuccessful attack on Hill 46, though the Battalion took no part in that attack. Had hill 46 been taken the enemy trenches in front of those occupied by the Battalion were to have	[illegible]

1247 W 3299 200,000 (E) 8/14 J.B.C. & A. Forms/C. 2118/11.

14

Instructions regarding War Diaries and Intelligence Summaries are contained in F. S. Regs., Part II. and the Staff Manual respectively. Title pages will be prepared in manuscript.

WAR DIARY
or
INTELLIGENCE SUMMARY
(Erase heading not required.)

Army Form C. 2118.

Hour, Date, Place	Summary of Events and Information	Remarks and references to Appendices
	been assaulted by troops from the 84th Bde who were brought into the trenches during the night of 12/13 for the purpose.	
March 19th	The Battalion left DRANOUTRE and marched to billets on the DRANOUTRE - NEUVE EGLISE road at BUS FARM and other farms.	
March 20th	A Draft of 133 accompanied by Capt. C. G. ~~GROVER~~ PHILLIPS and 2nd Lieut. K. W. S. OGLE arrived in DRANOUTRE and marched out to billets with the Battalion. The strength of the Battalion now became 849 all ranks.	
March 23rd	The Battalion proceeded to a further tour of duty in the trenches, relieving the E. Yorkshire Regt. and in the case of one Trench the York and Lancaster Regt.	

18

Instructions regarding War Diaries and Intelligence Summaries are contained in F. S. Regs., Part II. and the Staff Manual respectively. Title pages will be prepared in manuscript.

WAR DIARY
or
INTELLIGENCE SUMMARY
(Erase heading not required.)

Army Form C. 2118.

Hour, Date, Place	Summary of Events and Information	Remarks and references to Appendices
March 25th	A draft of 14 men arrived at NEUVE EGLISE, and joined their Companies on the 26th. The following Officers also arrived 2nd Lieuts. BROWN, MESNEY, CUTHBERTSON, TOMS, WINDELER the last 4 Officers attached from the R: Warwickshire Regt.	JEW
March 26th	Major CLOUGH arrived. The Companies in the fire trenches were relieved by those in the supporting post and farms.	v/A JEW
March 28th	~~The Battalion~~ A Draft of 69 men arrived, bringing the strength of the Battalion up to 29 Officers (including medical officer) and 897 other ranks.	JEW
March 29th	The Battalion was relieved in the trenches by the E. Yorkshire Regt. and marched to rest area near NEUVE EGLISE [being billeted in the huts]	JEW

19

Instructions regarding War Diaries and Intelligence Summaries are contained in F. S. Regs., Part II. and the Staff Manual respectively. Title pages will be prepared in manuscript.

WAR DIARY
or
INTELLIGENCE SUMMARY
(Erase heading not required.)

Army Form C. 2118.

Hour, Date, Place	Summary of Events and Information	Remarks and references to Appendices
	Known as ALDERSHOT CAMP.	
March 30th - 31st	In ALDERSHOT CAMP.	

1247 W 3299 200,000 (E) 8/14 J.B.C. & A. Forms/C. 2118/11.

83rd Bde.
28th Div.

WAR
DIARY

2nd K. O. R. LANCS.

APRIL.

1 9 1 6

28th Division

121/5609

2nd Royal Lancs

Vol III 1.4 — 3.5.15

3'S'
(8 sheets)

Confidential

War Diary of

2nd. Bn The King's Own Regt.

From 1. 4. 15. to 3. 5. 15.

Instructions regarding War Diaries and Intelligence Summaries are contained in F. S. Regs., Part II. and the Staff Manual respectively. Title pages will be prepared in manuscript.

WAR DIARY
or
INTELLIGENCE SUMMARY
(Erase heading not required.)

Army Form C. 2118.

Hour, Date, Place	Summary of Events and Information	Remarks and references to Appendices
~~[illegible]~~ April 1st NEUVE EGLISE	In huts at "ALDERSHOT" CAMP	
2 P.M. April 2nd NEUVE EGLISE	The Battalion [left NEUVE EGLISE and marched] to billets, in the neighbourhood of BOESCHEPE, [in 4 Farms and 3 small buildings]	
April 3rd – 8th	In Billets in neighbourhood of BOESCHEPE	
April 6th BOESCHEPE	A draft of 43 N.C.O.s & men arrived, bringing the strength of the Battalion up to 959.	
April 7th BOESCHEPE	The Battalion was inspected together with the remainder of the 83rd Infantry Brigade (2/ East Yorkshire Regt., 1/ York and Lancaster Regt., 1/ K.O. Yorkshire Light Infantry, 5/ The King's Own Regt., 3/ Monmouthshire Regt.)	

1247 W 3299 200,000 (E) 8/14 J.B.C. & A. Forms/C. 2118/11.

Army Form C. 2118.

Instructions regarding War Diaries and Intelligence Summaries are contained in F. S. Regs., Part II. and the Staff Manual respectively. Title pages will be prepared in manuscript.

WAR DIARY
or
INTELLIGENCE SUMMARY
(Erase heading not required.)

Hour, Date, Place	Summary of Events and Information	Remarks and references to Appendices
	by General Sir Horace Smith Dorien Commanding 2nd Army, who afterwards addressed the Officers of the Brigade and 3 N.C.O.s per Company	
3.P.M. April 8th BOESCHEPE	The Battalion [less A Company and Echelon B proceeded ~~marched~~] by motor bus to YPRES to billets in BOULEVARD MALOU	
12 noon	Echelon B and Transport proceed to YPRES by route march via WESTOUTRE. A Coy. remained in billets near BOESCHEPE	
12.30 P.M. April 9th YPRES	A Coy. rejoined the Battalion in YPRES by route march	
4.P.M. April 10th	The Commanding Officer, 2nd in Command, Adjutant and 2 Officers per Company proceeded to the trenches which were to be taken over by the Battalion, ~~[illegible]~~ when relieving	

1247 W 3299 200,000 (E) 8/14 J.B.C. & A. Forms/C. 2118/11.

Army Form C. 2118.

Instructions regarding War Diaries and Intelligence Summaries are contained in F. S. Regs., Part II. and the Staff Manual respectively. Title pages will be prepared in manuscript.

WAR DIARY
or
INTELLIGENCE SUMMARY
(Erase heading not required.)

Hour, Date, Place	Summary of Events and Information	Remarks and references to Appendices
	relieving] the 1 York and Lancaster Regt	
April 11th YPRES	In billets. A Draft of 24 N.C.Os. & men arrived bringing the strength of the Battalion up to 983	
9.P.M. April 12th	The Battalion [marched from YPRES by the MENIN Gate] to trenches of ZONNEBEKE. A, B, & C Companies occupied the trenches named F, G, H. while D Company was in reserve in "Dug outs" close to Battalion H. Qs. Though much work had been done since the York & Lancaster Regt. took over the trenches they were still very insecure and required much traversing and improvement of parapet.	
April 12th - April 16th	In trenches — D Company from the "Dug outs" relieved C Company in "H" trench on the evening of 14th.	

1247 W 3299 200,000 (E) 8/14 J.B.C. & A. Forms/C. 2118/11.

Instructions regarding War Diaries and Intelligence Summaries are contained in F. S. Regs., Part II. and the Staff Manual respectively. Title pages will be prepared in manuscript.

WAR DIARY
or
INTELLIGENCE SUMMARY
(Erase heading not required.)

Army Form C. 2118.

Hour, Date, Place	Summary of Events and Information	Remarks and references to Appendices
April 16th–17th	On night of April 16th–17th the Battalion was relieved by 1/York. Lancaster Regt. and returned to Billets in YPRES, [the last company arriving there shortly before 6. A. M.] During this tour in the trenches the Battalion lost 10 N.C.O.s & men killed and 9 wounded.	
11.45 A.M. April 17th YPRES	The Battalion marched from YPRES to billets and tents W. of VLAMERTINGHE. [on the VLAMERTINGHE – POPERINGHE road	
April 18th	In Billets and Camp	
	A draft of 50 arrived bringing the strength of the Battalion up to 1004	
April 19th	Remained in Billets	
2.15 P.M. April 20th	The Battalion marched to YPRES en route to trenches	

1247 W 3299 200,000 (E) 8/14 J.B.C. & A. Forms/C. 2118/11.

Instructions regarding War Diaries and Intelligence Summaries are contained in F. S. Regs., Part II. and the Staff Manual respectively. Title pages will be prepared in manuscript.

WAR DIARY
or
~~INTELLIGENCE SUMMARY~~
(Erase heading not required.)

Army Form C. 2118.

Hour, Date, Place	Summary of Events and Information	Remarks and references to Appendices
ZONNEBEKE. 20th april. 12 midnight.	On the march through YPRES the enemy heavily bombarded the town. One Officer and 20 men of C coy were wounded. One man killed. The Battalion took over the trenches from the YORK and LANCASTER Rgt. The trenches still required a lot of work before they could be considered safe.	JB.
21st April — 3rd May	Battalion in the trenches in front of ZONNEBEKE. During this period B. C. & D coys were heavily bombed on several occasions losing heavy casualties.	
3rd May. 10.30pm.	Orders were received for a general retirement. This was successfully carried out, simultaneously by Battalions, each trench leaving 1 officer & 20 men behind to cover the retirement. These men rejoined an hour afterwards. The Bn marched back through the North of YPRES to the huts W of the town. During this tour in the trenches the Casualties in the Bn were Officers 6 wounded O.R. 24 killed 142 wounded.	2/4th. JB.

83rd Bde.
28th Div.

2nd KING'S OWN ROYAL LANCS.

M A Y

1 9 1 5

Report on enemy attack
of FREZENBERG TRENCHES 8.5.15.

Confidential
War Diary
of
2nd. Bn The King's Own R. Regt.
From 4. 5. 15 To 28. 5. 15.
Volume 4.

Instructions regarding War Diaries and Intelligence Summaries are contained in F. S. Regs., Part II. and the Staff Manual respectively. Title pages will be prepared in manuscript.

WAR DIARY
or
INTELLIGENCE SUMMARY
(Erase heading not required.)

Army Form C. 2118.

Hour, Date, Place	Summary of Events and Information	Remarks and references to Appendices
Huts W of YPRES.	The Bn were resting in the huts.	
	The following reinforcements arrived on the 3rd May.	
4th May.	other ranks 240.	
7. pm	Orders were received to march out to the trenches and relieve the 5th Bn The Kings Own R.L.	
8.30 pm	The Bn marched out & took over trenches in front of FREZENBURG. The trenches were new trenches & had not been completed. A & D Coys were in the first line B & C Coys in support.	
	B Coy acting as support to the 3rd Monmouths.	
5th – 7th May.	Bn in the trenches. Enemy shelled trenches intermittently	
8th May. 7 am.	Enemy shelled trenches, blowing them in, and rendering them untenable. The enemy advanced and captured the front line trenches, they then advanced against the support dugouts. The O.C. 3rd Monmouths called for one company to support his line and B Coy	NS Cap

1247 W 3299 200,000 (E) 8/14 J.B.C. & A. Forms/C. 2118/11.

Army Form C. 2118.

Instructions regarding War Diaries and Intelligence Summaries are contained in F. S. Regs., Part II. and the Staff Manual respectively. Title pages will be prepared in manuscript.

WAR DIARY
or
INTELLIGENCE SUMMARY

(Erase heading not required.)

Hour, Date, Place	Summary of Events and Information	Remarks and references to Appendices
FREZENBURG. 8th May.	under Captain Forwood at once moved across the road and occupied some old Trenches E of the burial ground in rear of the Monmouth's Trenches.	
10. am.	Enemy commenced attack on the Supports dugouts but were held in check when 200 yds. from them.	
	The enemy were observed moving in a Westerly direction on both flanks of the position.	
	Major Clough assumed command on the death of Col. Martin.	
11.35 am.	Message received to retire on POTIJZE.	
	B Coy was ordered to retire first followed by the 3 platoons of C Coy. on the North of the YPRES – ZONNEBEKE road.	Attached messages + report marked X.
	The following Officers were present during the engagement.	
	Lt Col. A. R. S. Martin Killed	
	Major H.K. Clough	
	Captain C.W. Grover wounded + prisoner	
	Captain J.B. Forwood Killed.	[initials] Capt

1247 W 3299 200,000 (E) 8/14 J.B.C. & A. Forms/C. 2118/11.

Instructions regarding War Diaries and Intelligence Summaries are contained in F. S. Regs., Part II. and the Staff Manual respectively. Title pages will be prepared in manuscript.

WAR DIARY
or
INTELLIGENCE SUMMARY
(Erase heading not required.)

Army Form C. 2118.

Hour, Date, Place	Summary of Events and Information	Remarks and references to Appendices
8th May.	Lieut H.C.E. Jebb wounded	
	2/Lt. G.P.M. Scudamore missing	
	2/Lt Mesney. wounded	
	Lt Seddon wounded and prisoner	
	2/Lt Druchall killed.	
	2/Lt Horne hurt by fall.	
	2/Lt Brown wounded	
	2/Lt Somerville wounded	
	2/Lt Windeler missing	
	2/Lt Taylor. prisoner	
	Lt Rawlinson believed killed	
	Captain G E Weatherhead killed.	
	After the retirement regiments got mixed up. Some of the Bn retired back through the POTIJZE line and some remained in the trenches till the 9th May. Casualties of the Brigade Officers 128 O.R. 4379	[signature] Capt

1247 W 3299 200,000 (E) 8/14 J.B.C. & A. Forms/C. 2118/11.

Instructions regarding War Diaries and Intelligence Summaries are contained in F. S. Regs., Part II. and the Staff Manual respectively. Title pages will be prepared in manuscript.

WAR DIARY
or
INTELLIGENCE SUMMARY
(Erase heading not required.)

Army Form C. 2118.

Hour, Date, Place	Summary of Events and Information	Remarks and references to Appendices
9th May.	The remainder of the Battalion were withdrawn from the front line and sent back to the huts	
	The total casualties during this last tour in the trenches from 4th May till 9th May were:-	
	Officers. Killed 4 wounded 5 wounded & prisoners 2 wounded & missing 1 missing 4.	
	Other ranks. Killed 36 wounded 110 wounded & missing 31 missing 721.	
10th May. Huts W of YPRES.	Captain J. Bois took over command of the Bn from Major Clough.	
	The following officers arrived from England. Captain L. J. Cowper, Lt S. Long Innes. 2Lt Chesney.	
3 pm.	Orders were received to form the Brigade into a Composite Bn under Lt Colonel Worsley Gough of the 3rd Monmouths and proceed to the trenches at 7 pm. All men except a few of Echelon B. to be included.	Operation Orders. 10th May.

[illegible] Capt

1247 W 3299 200,000 (E) 8/14 J.B.C. & A. Forms/C. 2118/11.

Instructions regarding War Diaries and Intelligence Summaries are contained in F. S. Regs., Part II. and the Staff Manual respectively. Title pages will be prepared in manuscript.

WAR DIARY
or
INTELLIGENCE SUMMARY
(Erase heading not required.)

Army Form C. 2118.

Hour, Date, Place	Summary of Events and Information	Remarks and references to Appendices
10th May 7pm.	The Composite Bn proceeded to the Trenches. The men of the Battalion together with men of the YORK and LANCASTER Regt forming 1 company under Captain L. I. Cowper occupied the front line trenches by VERLOREN HOEK.	
11th May.	The Bn returned to the huts. Casualties NIL.	
10 pm.	The Bn moved to bivouacs nearer POPERINGHE.	
12th May.	The Bn moved nearer POPERINGHE and bivouacked in field.	
14th May.	The Brigade moved by bus to billets at STEENVOORDE	
	The Bn was billeted half way between STEENVOORDE and WINNEZEELE.	[illegible initials]
15th May	Resting	[illegible signature]

1247 W 3299 200,000 (E) 8/14 J.B.C. & A. Forms/C. 2118/11.

Army Form C. 2118.

Instructions regarding War Diaries and Intelligence Summaries are contained in F. S. Regs., Part II. and the Staff Manual respectively. Title pages will be prepared in manuscript.

WAR DIARY
or
INTELLIGENCE SUMMARY

(Erase heading not required.)

Hour, Date, Place	Summary of Events and Information		Remarks and references to Appendices
May 16th	Capt. Brammall joined the Battalion	Battalion in Billets between STEENVOORDE & WINNEZEELE	
May 17th	2/Lieut Jackson " "		
May 18th	Resting		
May 19th	Resting		
May 20th	Lieut Piers joined the Battalion		
	" Moore Williams " "		
	" Stevens " "		
	" Napier " "		
	" Best Dunkley " "		
	" Lawson Lewis " "		
	" Ravenscroft " "		
	" Lepper " "		
May 21st	Battalion Inspected by C in C Returned to bivouacs near VLAMINGTINGHE. O.C. Companies sent to trenches Reinforcements received 200.		
May 22nd	Battalion marched to the trenches 200 strong. The draft was left behind		

1247 W 3299 200,000 (E) 8/14 J.B.C. & A. Forms/C. 2118/11.

Instructions regarding War Diaries and Intelligence Summaries are contained in F. S. Regs., Part II. and the Staff Manual respectively. Title pages will be prepared in manuscript.

WAR DIARY
or
INTELLIGENCE SUMMARY

(Erase heading not required.)

Army Form C. 2118.

Hour, Date, Place	Summary of Events and Information	Remarks and references to Appendices
May 22nd 10.30 pm	The Battalion took over two Trenches in front of SANCTUARY WOOD from Royal Irish Regiment	
	5th Kings Own on our left. 2nd East Yorks on our right.	
May 23rd – 24th	In the Trenches. Intermittent Shelling	
May 24th 3.am	Enemy attacked Cavalry on our left preceded by Gas. Enemy broke through South of the MENIN ROAD	
6.am	2 Companies York & Lancaster Regiment, who were in Support dugouts made a Counter attack through ZUAVE WOOD and drove enemy North of MENIN Road	
May 25th – 31st	Battalion in the Trenches. Enemy shelled the trenches intermittently every day	
May 27th	Reinforcements joined the Battalion i.e.	
	2 Capt Hebbert	
	Morrell	
	2 Lt O'Brien	
	Milner and 199 other Ranks	
May 28th	Lieut Bennett joined the Battalion with a draft of 132 other Ranks	

1247 W 3299 200,000 (E) 8/14 J.B.C. & A. Forms/C. 2118/11.

Report on attack

Frezenberg

by Enemy

8.5.15

X [illegible]

Headquarters
Brd. Brigade

I have the honour to submit the following report on the attack on the FRANZENBERG line of trenches held by the 2nd. Bn The King's Own Regiment on Saturday May 8th 1915.

Two Companies D and A under Lieut Jebb and Captain Grover held those trenches North of the YPRES – ZONNEBEKE road and one platoon of C Company under Lieut. Horne held a section of trench on the South of the road. The 3rd. Monmouth Regt. continued the line south. 'B' Coy. and 3 platoons of C Coy. were in support occupying dugouts.

The enemy began to bombard the Fire Trenches between 7 and 8 a.m. and continued until about 10 a.m. destroying the parapets and rendering the trenches untenable. I am unable to definitely account for any N.C.Os. and men from the Fire Trenches.

On the cessation of the bombardment the enemy seized the trenches and advanced to attack the support dugouts. At this juncture the O.C. 3rd. Monmouths called for one company to support his line and accordingly B Coy. under Captain

Forwood at once moved forward and occupied some old earthworks on the E. side of a burial ground in rear of the Monmouth Trenches being unable to advance further. About 10 a.m. the attack on the Battalion support dugouts began, the enemy having advanced to within about 200 yards of them, where they were held in check.

In the meantime considerable numbers of the enemy could be seen moving in a westerly direction on both flanks of the position.

Colonel Martin was killed very soon after the attack on the dugouts began and Captain & Adjutant Weatherhead was severely wounded in the head.

Lt. Mitchell was also killed at an early stage of the attack.

I assumed command of the Battalion.

At this juncture the situation in front was favourable, the enemy making no attempt to advance - however on both flanks heavy rifle & machine gun fire was opened against my position. I, however, had comparatively few casualties. At 11.35 a.m. I received the following message:-

O.C. King's Own

Brigade Order just arrived in the form of a message from O.C. East Yorks to Adjutant who is now with us. Retire on POTIJZE and hold on at all costs.

Signed W. Ramsden, Captn & Adjt. 3rd. Mons.

I accordingly sent a message to the Officer Commanding B Company ordering him to retire and directing him to make the best of his way back to the POTIZZE line avoiding the main road.

I then made arrangements to withdraw the 3 platoons I had directly under my orders. This was a most difficult operation and as I expected resulted in heavy casualties – only 40 N.C.Os. & men succeeding in reaching the POTIZZE line with me.

Immediately I began to withdraw the enemy rushed the position I had held and opened a heavy rifle & machine gun fire from the position and on both my flanks their guns also opened fire with shrapnel & high explosive shells.

Captn. Weatherhead was killed by shrapnel when within a few yards of the Potize line of trenches.

The following Officers were present during the engagement:–

Lt. Col. A. R. S. Martin. Killed
Major H. K. Clough.
Captn. C. W. Groves. Wounded & missing believed killed.
Captn. J. B. Farwood. Killed
Lieut H. C. E. Jebb. wounded.
2/Lt. G. J. M. Scudamore. missing.
" Mooney. wounded.
Lt. Seddon wounded & missing.
2/Lt. Muchall. Killed.
" Horne. hurt by a fall.
" Brown. Wounded.
" Sommerville. wounded (at duty)
" Windeler. Missing.
" Taylor. Missing

Lieut. Rawlinson, believed buried in
Fire Trench.

Captn & Adjt Weatherhead, killed.

I wish to bring to your notice the gallant conduct of Captain Weatherhead who though severely wounded refused to leave me as he could have done in safety at the time he was wounded. He was the greatest assistance to me in holding the line of dugouts. He also refused to remain behind when the retirement began, but insisted in accompanying me & rendering me what assistance was possible during the retirement, thereby losing his life.

As far as can be ascertained the casualties amongst N.C.Os & men amounted to 922.

Major

Commdg. 1st The King's Own Regt.

11th May 1915.

Hd. Qrs 83rd Bde X 2/4

Please see attached report sent to Observing Officer [illegible] Battery R.F.A. With reference to situation S of FREZENBERG my Platoon and left of Monmouths have been heavily shelled today — by H.E. & shrapnel & yesterday. I had 8 men & 1 officer wounded in that Platoon — today I hear there are 12 casualties in my Platoon but communication is now cut and I cannot verify — The Monmouths say their left is similarly suffering — As my Platoon is in Monmouth Artillery sector I have asked OC that Batty. to call for support from our Artillery when required. I think that Howitzers should send up observation officer and destroy houses, razing them to the ground, ie houses in front of ~~[illegible]~~ centre sector in front of our line on the South side of the YPRES-ZONNEBEKE Road — these houses are I believe occupied by the enemy, as I thought shots came from them last night when I visited the line —

I cannot get a full report until I relieve my Platoon S of the Road tonight.

If these houses are not destroyed by Artillery it is possible that they may in the future conceal snipers who will enfilade the line in both directions, and possibly they are already used as hostile artillery observation stations, although the enemy have plenty of other commanding positions from which to observe —

If this house was bombarded, an Artillery Officer knowing the range at which guns for this purpose would be placed, and knowing the safe distance for Infantry, would decide whether it would be necessary to withdraw my Infantry from the trenches — I think Machine Guns could cover the unoccupied space if placed on my ~~right~~ [illegible] and on Monmouths left — I would reoccupy the trench with my platoon as soon as the road is cut through; this work is in progress and should be completed tonight —

4 p.m
7.5.15

A.R.S. Martin Lt Col
Comdr 2/ Kings Own Rgt.

Cannot an aeroplane be asked to come & any Battery be allowed to reconnoitre the ~~and~~ Enemys heavy guns and to observe for ours —

JS Capt

To Observation Officer 62nd Batty RFA

ZONNEBEKE

Germans

200x

900

British

FREZENBERG

To YPRES

The above sketch is drawn up from reports of officers in the fire trenches — It shows roughly the position of the Germans on the front defended by 2/ Kings Own (Capt Dickson of 83rd Inf Bde). The Germans are apparently digging parallels by night and then gradually approaching our lines, but I cannot say which trenches they occupy by day, probably those more distant from us until they have completed the more advanced trenches.

2.25 p.m.

9.5.15

A R S Martin Lt-Col

Comdg 2/ Kings Own Regt

J.B. Capt

"C" Form (Original).

Army Form C. 2123.

MESSAGES AND SIGNALS.

No. of Message

Prefix Code Words

Received From By

Sent, or sent out At m. To By

Office Stamp.

£ s. d

Charges to collec

Service Instructions.

Handed in at Office m. Received m.

TO O.C. 2 Kings Own

*Sender's Number	Day of Month	In reply to Number	AAA
E.Y. 6	5		

Enemy	are	attacking	my	right
company	in	force	and	I
have	used	up	all	my
supports	aaa	My	right	is
at	ARRET	J I A b		aaa
Will	you	have	supports	ready
at	once	in	case	they
are	wanted.	aaa	I have informed brigade	

H Powell Maj
OC 2/Yorks R

5.5.15 10.25 am

FROM pp Capt

PLACE & TIME

* This line should be erased if not required.

W.2384—583. 30,000 Pads - 8/14. S. B. Ltd. Forms/C.2123.

"A" Form. Army Form C. 2121.

MESSAGES AND SIGNALS.

No. of Message

Code m. Office of Origin and Service Instructions	Words / Charge / Sent At m To By	This message is on a/c of: Service. (Signature of "Franking Officer.")	Recd. at 340 P.m. Date From By

TO 2/Kings Own

Sender's Number.	Day of Month.	In reply to Number	
Sc 62	Fifth		AAA

Let me know approximate strength of your trench as soon as possible

A 238
B 110 / 112 3
C 246 3
D 243 4
949

Officers 14

[signature] Capt

From Eighty Third Bde
Place
Time 2.50 p.m.

The above may be forwarded as now corrected.

Censor.

(Z) E C Applayard

Signature of Addressor or person authorised to telegraph in his name.

* This line should be erased if not required.

(75614). Wt. 11400-2045. 50,000. 2-15. B, M. & S, Ltd.

"A" Form. Army Form C. 2121.

MESSAGES AND SIGNALS. No. of Message

Prefix .... Code .... m. | Words | Charge

Office of Origin and Service Instructions: LHC

Sent: At .... m. To .... By ....

This message is on a/c of: .... Service.

(Signature of "Franking Officer.")

Recd. at .... m. Date LHC From By 5/5/15

TO { Monmouth
Second Kings Own

Sender's Number.	Day of Month.	In reply to Number	
* BM 90	Fifth		AAA

If	O.C.	Monmouth	does	not
consider	himself	strong	enough	to
hold	the	whole	line	from
the	railway	to	the	YPRES
ZONNEBEKE		road	he	will
inform	O.C.	Second	Kings	Own
who	will	then	take	over
the	left	~~part~~	part	as
far	as	two	hundred	yards
from	the	road	if	necessary
AAA	Monmouth	will	not	find
any	supports	therefore	Kings	Own
will	be	prepared	to	support
Monmouth	if	called	on	by
O.C.	Monmouth			

JB Capt

From 83 Bde
Place
Time 10 pm

The above may be forwarded as now corrected. (Z) J. S. Munby Capt

Censor. Signature of Addressor or person authorised to telegraph in his name.

* This line should be erased if not required.

11400-2345. 50,000. 2-15. B. M. & S. Ltd.

83rd Bde.
28th Division.

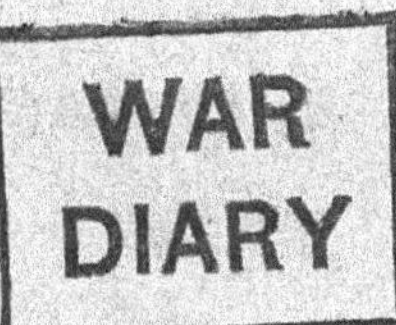

2nd KING'S OWN ROYAL LANCS.

J U N E

1 9 1 5

Instructions regarding War Diaries and Intelligence Summaries are contained in F. S. Regs., Part II. and the Staff Manual respectively. Title pages will be prepared in manuscript.

WAR DIARY
or
INTELLIGENCE SUMMARY

(Erase heading not required.)

Army Form C. 2118.

Hour, Date, Place	Summary of Events and Information	Remarks and references to Appendices
June 1st – 2nd	Battalion in the trenches. Intermittent shelling by whizz-bangs & 5" shells.	
June 2nd 5 am	Enemy started heavy bombardment of Cavalry trenches in HOOGE VILLAGE and CHATEAU and in front of ZOUAVE WOOD. Bombardment lasted until 5.30 pm with a break at 12 noon.	
	Enemy shelled our trenches heavily about 10 am and again at 2.30 pm	
12 midnight	Battalion relieved by Northumberland Fusiliers and returned to huts at OUDERDON	
	Casualties during last tour:–	
	Officers wounded – Captain Bois	
	O.R. killed – 2	
	wounded – 20	
June 3rd 4 am	Battalion arrived in huts at OUDERDON	
1.30 pm	Battalion marched to Billets at BRIEL near WINNEZEELE	
5.0 pm	Battalion arrived at Billets	[signature] Capt

1247 W 3299 200,000 (E) 8/14 J.B.C. & A. Forms/C. 2118/11.

Instructions regarding War Diaries and Intelligence Summaries are contained in F. S. Regs., Part II. and the Staff Manual respectively. Title pages will be prepared in manuscript.

WAR DIARY
or
INTELLIGENCE SUMMARY
(Erase heading not required.)

Army Form C. 2118.

Hour, Date, Place	Summary of Events and Information	Remarks and references to Appendices
4th June	Lieut T.R. Blaum joined the Battalion	
4th June – 14th June	Battalion in Reserve in Billets at WINNEZEELE	
6th June	Major J.C. Borrett } Lieut V.L. de Cordova } rejoined	
	Reinforcements 24 other Ranks	
11th June	Reinforcements 25 other Ranks	
1.15 pm 14th June	The Battalion moved from Billet in WINNEZEELE by march route to Huts near ZEVECOTON	
7. pm. 14th June	The Battalion arrived at the Huts near ZEVECOTON	
15th June – 18th June	In huts at ZEVECOTON in Reserve	
18th June	Reinforcements O.R. 47 in Reserve	
19th June	In Huts at ZEVECOTON in reserve	
1.30 pm 20th June	The Battalion moved from Huts ZEVECOTON by march route to Billets in LOCRE	
3.0 pm " "	Battalion arrived in Billets in LOCRE. Lieut E.K.T. Tucker joined the Battalion	
8.45 pm " "	Carrying party of 2 officers & 200 other Ranks proceeded to the trenches	
2.30 am 21st June	Carrying party returned. Casualties O.R. wounded one	
	Battalion in billets LOCRE in reserve	J.[illegible] Capt

1247 W 3299 200,000 (E) 8/14 J.B.C. & A. Forms/C. 2118/11.

Army Form C. 2118.

Instructions regarding War Diaries and Intelligence Summaries are contained in F. S. Regs., Part II. and the Staff Manual respectively. Title pages will be prepared in manuscript.

WAR DIARY
or
INTELLIGENCE SUMMARY
(Erase heading not required.)

Hour, Date, Place	Summary of Events and Information	Remarks and references to Appendices
June 22nd	Battalion in Billets at LOCRE	
8.45 pm	Working Party of 300 & Carrying party of 100 for 7/E. Yorks	
3. am June 23rd	Working & Carrying party returned. Casualties O.R. one wounded	
9. am " "	CO. Adjutant & all Company Commanders & M.G.O. proceeded to reconnoitre Trenches	
8. pm " "	Battalion marched out of Billets at LOCRE en route to relieve 1st York & Lancs in the Trenches in front of KEMMEL (83rd Bde Operation Order No 37).	
	B.C.&D Coys in fire trenches & support. A Coy: in Reserve	
	Trenches occupied: K1b on the right to L.7. on the left, on VIERSTRAAT–WYTSCHAETE Road. Reserve Company two Platoons in SANDBAG VILLA & surrounding barns; two Platoons in Brigade Dugouts & VIERSTRAAT with two M.G.s	
	Battalion H.Q. at HOWITZER FARM	
1. am June 24th	Relief Complete.	
4.30 pm "	Situation Quiet. Casualties wounded O.R. one.	
10 pm June 24th	Two Platoons of Reserve Coy (A Coy) handed over Brigade Dugouts & VIERSTRAAT to 2 Northumberland Fusiliers of 84th Brigade. One M.G. withdrawn from Brigade Dugouts one M.G. left at VIERSTRAAT.	
11.30 am June 25th	Bn. H.Q. moved from HOWITZER FARM to YORK HOUSE	
12. noon " "	Casualties ~~during~~ previous 24 hours O.R. ~~Killed~~ two.	
2. pm " "	Slight shelling of trenches L4 & 5 & Support Trenches otherwise quiet.	
8.30 pm "	Following reliefs carried out: One M.G. at VIERSTRAAT relieved by 84th Brigade M.G.	
June 26th	Battalion in the trenches, Lieuts. S.E. Sowill, & D.A. Ballard joined the Battalion.	
12. noon "	Casualties previous 24 hours O.R. Killed one, wounded four.	
	Situation quiet slight shelling of L4 & support trenches.	
June 27th	Battalion in the trenches. Situation Quiet. Casualties previous 24 hours nil.	

1247 W 3299 200,000 (E) 8/14 J.B.C. & A. Forms/C. 2118/11.

Instructions regarding War Diaries and Intelligence Summaries are contained in F. S. Regs., Part II. and the Staff Manual respectively. Title pages will be prepared in manuscript.

WAR DIARY
or
INTELLIGENCE SUMMARY
(Erase heading not required.)

Army Form C. 2118.

Hour, Date, Place	Summary of Events and Information	Remarks and references to Appendices
June 28th	Battalion in the trenches Situation quiet up to 2.15 pm when began shelling slightly from left to right of Bn. Trenches about sixty shells in all came over of various Calibre Casualties during previous 24 hours O.R. wounded slightly at duty 1	
June 29th	Battalion in the trenches Situation quiet except for intermittent shelling Casualties during previous 24 hours Officers wounded two (Lieut F.C. Naper seriously, Lieut S. Long Innes slightly and at duty) O.R. killed one, wounded 9.	
10 pm June 29th	Under Brigade Operation Order No 40 the Battalion was relieved in the trenches by 1st York & Lancs.	
11.45 pm "	Relief complete and Battalion march to huts at SCHERPENBERG. near LA CLYTTE	[illegible]
3. am June 30th	The Battalion arrived at Huts at SCHERPENBERG.	

1247 W 3299 200,000 (E) 8/14 J.B.C. & A. Forms/C. 2118/11.

83rd Bde.
28th Div.

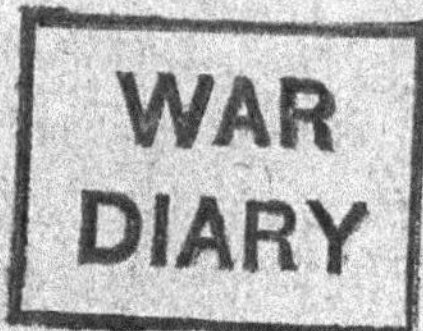

2nd KING'S OWN ROYAL LANCS.

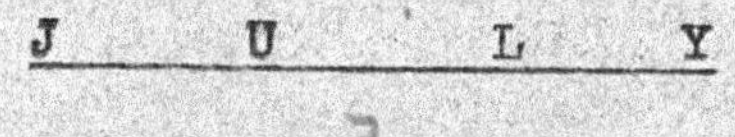

J U L Y

1 9 1 5

Confidential

War Diary

— of —

2nd. Bn. The King's Own Regiment.

From 1. 7. 15 to 31. 7. 15.

— Vol. 6. —

Army Form C. 2118.

Instructions regarding War Diaries and Intelligence Summaries are contained in F. S. Regs., Part II. and the Staff Manual respectively. Title pages will be prepared in manuscript.

WAR DIARY
or
INTELLIGENCE SUMMARY
(Erase heading not required.)

Hour, Date, Place	Summary of Events and Information	Remarks and references to Appendices
1st July – 5th July	Battalion in Huts at SCHERPENBERG Casualties during this period O.R. wounded one.	
9.30pm 5th July	The Battalion relieved the 1st York & Lancs in the same trenches as last time under Brigade Operation Order No [illegible] Companies in the trenches C. D & B with A Coy in reserve. Relief completed [illegible] pm.	
6 July	In the trenches. Lieut Col. [illegible] assumed command of the Battalion from [illegible] Capt. Casualties up to 12 noon O.R. wounded [illegible]	
10pm July 6th	Following relief took place A Coy relieved D Coy in [illegible] trenches. D Coy moving into Reserve	
1am July 7th	Above relief complete. Battalion in the trenches. Casualties up to noon O.R. wounded four.	
July 8th	Battalion in the trenches. Casualties up to 12 noon O.R. wounded three	
July 9th	Battalion in the trenches. Casualties up to 12 noon O.R. wounded one. Reinforcements Captain C. G. Phillips & 17 O.R.	
July 10th	Battalion in the trenches. Casualties up to 12 noon O.R. killed one wounded one	
4pm [illegible] pm July 10	Slight shelling of [illegible] trenches. No damage done except [illegible] was blown in. [illegible] without any effect.	
July 11th	Battalion in the trenches. Casualties up to 12 noon O.R. killed one wounded one	[illegible] Capt & Adjt

1247 W 3299 200,000 (E) 8/14 J.B.C. & A. Forms/C. 2118/11.

Instructions regarding War Diaries and Intelligence Summaries are contained in F. S. Regs., Part II. and the Staff Manual respectively. Title pages will be prepared in manuscript.

WAR DIARY
or
INTELLIGENCE SUMMARY
(Erase heading not required.)

Army Form C. 2118.

Hour, Date, Place	Summary of Events and Information	Remarks and references to Appendices
10 pm July 11th	Battalion relieved in the trenches by 1st Bn. York & Lancaster Regt. Relief complete 11.45 pm.	
July 12th	Battalion at rest at SCHERPENBERG. Companies occupying same huts as when at rest last time. [illegible] O.C. Barrett [illegible]	
July 13th–14	Battalion at Rest. Casualties up to [illegible] 13th O.R. wounded one.	
July 14th	Casualties up to 12 noon O.R. wounded two, [illegible] the Germans exploding a mine in [illegible] 43. The Battalion [illegible] 9.30 pm [illegible] move off at 10.30 pm. [illegible] relieved 11.45 pm	
8 pm July 15th	The Battalion left SCHERPENBERG to relieve 1st Suffolk Regt in the Trenches. The Battalion occupies the same Trenches as last time with the exception of K1.b & K2. which are held by one Company 1/5 Kings Own under command of O.C. Kings Own. Relief complete 12.10 am 16/7/15	
July 16th	Battalion in the trenches. Situation quiet. Slight shelling in the afternoon. Casualties O.R. Killed 1. wounded 2.	
July 17th	Battalion in the trenches, weather bad and interfered with work. The following	
9.30 pm	relief was carried out 1 Officer (Lieut [illegible]) and one Platoon of 50 O.R. relieved 1/5 Kings Own in K1.b & K2. Casualties up to midday O.R. wounded 3.	
July 18th	Battalion in the trenches. Situation quiet except for intermittent [illegible] of the L. trenches by the enemy. Casualties up to midday O.R. killed 1 wounded [illegible].	
July 19th	Battalion in the trenches. Situation quiet. In the evening the enemy shelled Farm Parrett and the Subsidiary Line, they seem to pay [illegible] particular attention to this line. Casualties up to midday O.R. wounded 1. The following officers attached to the Battalion from the Lancashire Fusiliers were transferred to their own Regt. Lieuts. Best [illegible], Rawcroft, [illegible] Lewis 2Lieut Pepper.	[illegible] Capt Adjt

1247 W 3299 200,000 (E) 8/14 J.B.C. & A. Forms/C. 2118/11.

Instructions regarding War Diaries and Intelligence Summaries are contained in F. S. Regs., Part II. and the Staff Manual respectively. Title pages will be prepared in manuscript.

WAR DIARY
or
INTELLIGENCE SUMMARY
(Erase heading not required.)

Army Form C. 2118.

Hour, Date, Place	Summary of Events and Information	Remarks and references to Appendices
July 20th	Battalion in the Trenches. Situation quiet. Casualties up to midday Nil.	
" 21st	Battalion in the trenches. Situation quiet. Casualties up to midday O.R. wounded 1	
10. pm	Relief of the Battalion commenced by ½ [illegible] in all the L. Trenches, K.2 b and K.3. and also at York House [illegible] By the 1st K.O.Y.L.I. in K.1 b, K.2, K.2 a by 1st York & Lancasters at [illegible]	
11.30 pm " "	Relief complete, and the Battalion moved by companies to the Huts at LA CLYTTE	
3.30 pm July 22nd	Battalion moved from huts LA CLYTTE into Bivouacs at SCHERPENBERG to make room for 17th Division	
7.45 pm July 23rd	Battalion moved from Bivouacs into Huts at SCHERPENBERG vacated by by 1st York & Lancasters.	
8.0 pm	Two Officers (Lieut Blair & Lieut [illegible]) + 100 O.R. provided to [illegible] to relieve 1st York & Lancasters.	
July 24th	Battalion at rest. The following reinforcements arrived O.R. 59	
July 25th – 28th	Battalion at rest. The following Casualty occurred on 28th. O.R. wounded 1	
1. pm July 29th	The Battalion moved from Huts at SCHERPENBERG to take over the C Trenches in front of WULVERGEM, Relieving the 1st East Yorkshire Regt.	
July 30th & 31st	The Battalion in the Trenches.	
		J. R. B[illegible] Capt & Adjt

1247 W 3299 200,000 (E) 8/14 J.B.C. & A. Forms/C. 2118/11.

83rd Bde.
28th Division.

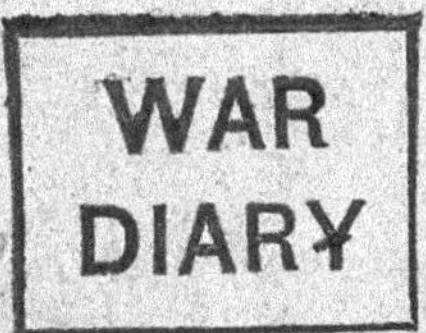

2nd KING'S OWN ROYAL LANCS.

A U G U S T

1 9 1 5

Confidential
War Diary
— of —
2nd Bn: The King's Own Regt.

From 1. 8. 15 To 31. 8. 1915.

Volume V.

Instructions regarding War Diaries and Intelligence Summaries are contained in F. S. Regs., Part II. and the Staff Manual respectively. Title Pages will be prepared in manuscript.

WAR DIARY
or
INTELLIGENCE SUMMARY
(Erase heading not required.)

Army Form C. 2118

Place	Date	Hour	Summary of Events and Information	Remarks and references to Appendices
WOLVERGHEM	Aug 1st		Battalion in the Trenches. The following reinforcements arrived O.R. 48	APP. I
"	Aug 2nd		" " "	
"	" 3rd		" " " " Casualties O.R. Killed 1.	
"	" 4th		" " " " Casualties Officers Killed 1 (Lieut. S. Long Innes) O.R. Killed 1. Wounded 2.	
"	" 5th	11.0 pm	Battalion relieved in the Trenches by 2nd Bn The Buffs and proceeded into Bivouacs at SCHERPENBERG. During the above time we were under the 85th Brigade.	APP. 2.
SCHERPENBERG	6th		Battalion at rest. The following reinforcements arrived O.R. 50	
"	Aug 7th–10th		" " " Casualties O.R. wounded 1 on 7-8-15	
"	Aug 11th	7.45 pm	Battalion moved from SCHERPENBERG bivouacs & relieved 1st Bn York & Lancaster Regt in the Trenches of Right Sector, Ref. Ho., in front of KEMMEL. One Company of 6th Leicesters attached to Battalion for instruction for the trenches for 48 hours. Two Companies of 1/3 Kings Own occupying H Trenches came under command of O.C. Battalion.	app. 3.
KEMMEL	Aug 12th		In the Trenches. Casualties up to midday O.R. wounded 2. The Company of 6th Leicester Regt attached to the Battn were withdrawn at dusk after only 24 hours.	app. 4.
"	Aug 13th		Battn in the Trenches. The enemy shelled KEMMEL Village dropping 10 shells in it about 4.30 pm. They also dropped shells behind our support trenches: no damage done. Casualties up to midday O.R. wounded 2.	
		9.30 pm	Two Companies 6th Leicester Regt relieved two Companies 1/3 Kings Own & came under the command of O.C. the Battn.	
"	Aug 14th		Battn in the Trenches. The enemy again dropped a few shells behind our Support Trenches no damage done. Casualties O.R. wounded 1. Reinforcements O.R. 19	
"	Aug 15	3.30 pm	Battn in the Trenches. Our Artillery bombarded PETIT BOIS opposite the K trenches where the enemy had has been making some new works, material damage done unknown.	
		4.30 pm	An Intelligence Officer got into Communication with the enemy opposite our trenches and obtained their Newspapers & other information from which it was ascertained that troops opposite us were 18th Regt of 2nd Bavarian Division. Casualties up to midday O.R. wounded 2.	
"	Aug 16th		Battn in the Trenches. Casualties O.R. Killed 1.	
"	Aug 17th	11.20 pm	Battn Relieved in the Trenches by 1st Bn York & Lancaster Regt and returned to SCHERPENBERG bivouacs. Owing to the Brigade taking over the Q. Trenches from 84th Brigade on our [illegible], on our relief what was the right Sub of Brigade area became the left.	App. 5.

1875 Wt. W593/826 1,000,000 4/15 J.B.C. & A. A.D.S.S./Forms/C. 2118.

Instructions regarding War Diaries and Intelligence Summaries are contained in F. S. Regs., Part II. and the Staff Manual respectively. Title Pages will be prepared in manuscript.

WAR DIARY
or
INTELLIGENCE SUMMARY
(Erase heading not required.)

Army Form C. 2118

Place	Date	Hour	Summary of Events and Information	Remarks and references to Appendices
SCHERPENBERG	Aug 18th	11.30am	Battn at Rest. The Battalion together with a detachment of R.F.A. and 11th Bn. The Suffolk Regt of 84th Brigade were inspected at SCHERPENBERG by H.H. The Earl Kitchener of Khartoum, Secretary of State for War; and the French War Minister.	
"	Aug 19th – 22nd		Battalion at Rest. ~~Reinforcements~~	
"	Aug 23rd		Under Brigade O.O. The Battalion relieved the 1st Bn. York & Lancaster Regt in the Trenches of Centre Sector. On relief being complete part of the Garrison of 13 Trench (25 O.R. 3rd Monmouth Regt) came under the orders of O.C. Battalion. Reinforcements one Officer Lieut D.E. Markland	Bde O.O. No 65. & Battn. O.O. No 20 — app 6
KEMMEL	Aug 24th	4. pm	Battn in the Trenches. The enemy dropped H.E. 8" shells behind the Support Trenches no damage done. Casualties up to midday O.R. wounded (slightly at duty).	
"	Aug 25th	4 pm	Battn in the Trenches. Enemy ~~dropped~~ H.E. 5.9 Shells between K.1 & K1a Trenches doing little damage to Parapet.	
		7.45pm	The Enemy exploded a Mine in front of the left of I.3 Right no damage was done to our parapet or Gallery.	
		8. pm	The enemy attacked I.3 Right with bombs & hand grenades which lasted for about 15 minutes, about 60 bombs & hand grenades were thrown into the trench doing little or no material damage. Our Artillery opened fire and the attack ceased. All was quiet for the remainder of the night. As a result of the above attack the following casualties occurred:- Officers wounded 2 (Lieuts Blair & Chesney) O.R. wounded 8	
"	Aug 26th / 29		Battalion in the Trenches. The enemy shelled behind the Support Trenches daily doing no damage. The enemy are very busy working on their line in PETIT BOIS opposite our Trenches. The Artillery shelled their working parties & the Howitzer Battery shelled their works, but what damage was done is unknown. Casualties for this period O.R. wounded 5. The following reinforcements arrived on 26th 2Lt W.A.L. Thorne & 2Lt Andrews	
	Aug 29th	9.40pm	The Battalion relieved in the Centre Sector by 1st Bn. York & Lancaster Regt. On Completion of Relief the Battn. returned to Bivouacs at SCHERPENBERG	app 7.
SCHERPENBERG	Aug 30th		Battn at Rest. 700 men sent out on working parties during day & night. Reinforcements Lieut W.S. Ellis & Lieut R.M. Philipson-Stow	
"	Aug 31st	2. pm	The Battn was inspected by the G.O.C. 2nd Army. The following is the Sick Wastage in the Battalion during the month of August: 44. Rejoined Bn from Hos 26.	

1875 Wt. W593/826 1,000,000 4/15 J.B.C. & A. A.D.S.S./Forms/C. 2118.

App I File

OPERATION ORDERS NO. 24
By Lieut. Colonel E.M. Morris,
Commdg. 2nd. Bn. The King's Own Regiment.

THURSDAY. 29.7.1915.

The Battalion will move from SCHERPENBERG at 1 p.m. today and proceed to the trenches.
Order of March :-

A Company.
C Company.
B Company.
D Company.
2Lt. G.L.Chesney's Party.

Machine Gunners and Signallers will move off at 12.45 p.m.
The Battalion will halt in a field near DRANOUTRE for the evening meal.
Machine Gunners & Signallers will relieve during daylight, under special orders.
The Battalion will resume march from the field and will march as such to BUS FARM and from thence by Coys. at five minutes interval.
Guides for each Company will meet the Battalion at BUS FARM and conduct Coys. to Battn. Headquarters where guides to the trenches will be provided.
The Battalion will occupy trenches as detailed below :-

A Coy. - C.1. 84 men.
C.2. 58 men. TOTAL 142 men.
B Coy. - Diagonal Trench 160 men.
C Coy. - ~~A.~~ C.3. 108 men.
C.3. Support. 41 men. TOTAL. 149 men.
D Coy. - C.4. 80 men.
C.4. Support. 38 men.
S.P.4. 15 men. TOTAL 133 men.

2Lt. Chesney's Party will consist of :-
A Coy. 30 men.
C Coy. 18 men.
D Coy. 30 men. TOTAL 78.

This ~~E~~ party will be the Battalion support at SOUVENIER FARM and NORTH MIDLAND FARM, divided as follows :-
1 Officer & 58 men at SOUVENIER FARM.
20 men at NORTH MIDLAND FARM.

Battalion Headquarters will be at ST. QUINTEN FARM.
Dressing Station near Battalion Headquarters.

Trench garrisons will be told off before leaving SCHERPENBERG and will march off.

Distribution reports to reach Battalion Headquarters by 4 a.m. tomorrow.

Starting Point for march - 100 yards short of the WESTOUTRE CROSS ROADS.

The Battalion while in these trenches will be under the 85th. Bde.

Sd. C.C. BORRETT, Major for Adjutant.
2nd. Bn. The King's Own Regiment.

NOTE - Billets are to be left clean before leaving.

OPERATION ORDER Nº 11 COPY Nº 7

By Brig-General C.E. PEREIRA, App 2.

Commanding 85d Inf. Brigade.

1/8/1915.

1. On the night of the 4/5 August the 84th Inf. Bde will extend to its right and will take over from 85d Inf Bde the trenches at present held by the 2/East Surrey Regt.

2. 2/East Surrey Regt will on relief move into billets which will be notified later.

3. On the night of the 5/6 August the 2/The Buffs will take over the trenches at present occupied by the 2/King's Own Regt. (C trenches).

4. The O.C. 2/The Buffs will send up 1 officer per company and 1 guide per platoon to reconnoitre the C trenches on the 4th August at an hour to be fixed between Commanding Officers. The platoon guides will remain in the trenches.

5. O.C. Coys of 2/The Buffs will go into the trenches at 2 p.m. on the 5d.

6.

6 After the re-adjustment of the line points of junction between Brigades will be as follows:

Between Canadian Divn. and 85th Inf. Bde. }	Trench C1 inclusive to 85th Inf. Bde.
Between 85th Inf. Bde. and 84th Inf. Bde. }	Trench D4 inclusive to 85th Inf. Bde.

7 The C.O. under whose command the trenches now are, will remain in command until reliefs are complete.

8. O.C. Battalions will report to 85th Inf. Bde. Headquarters the hour at which relief is completed.

J Howe Capt
Bde Major 85th Inf Bde

Copy No 1 retained
2 84th Inf. Bde.
3 2/ The Buffs
4 2/ E. Surrey Regt
5 3/ Royal Fusiliers
6 3/ Middlesex Regt.
7 2/ King's Own.

App 3. Tile

OPERATION ORDER NO. 26.
By Lieut. Colonel E.M. Morris,
Commdg. 2nd. Bn. The King's Own Regiment,

WEDNESDAY. 11.8.1915

The Battalion will relieve the 1st. Bn. York & Lancaster Regt. tonight, in the RIGHT SECTOR.

Coys. will move off in the following order at 5 minutes interval, commencing with "D" Coy. at 7.45 p.m. and occupy trenches as shown :-

(i) "D" Coy. (K.1. (K.1.A. (K.1.U. NEW (S.P.13.

(ii) "A" Coy. (J.3. Right. (J.3. Left. (J.3.U. NEW (J.4. (J.11. (S.P.12.

(iii) "B" Coy. (H.3.4 (J.1. (J.2. (J.10.

(iv) "C" Coy. -SIEGE FARM.

Bn. H.Qrs. - ROSSIGNOL ESTAMINET.

Guides will meet D. A. and B Coys. at the LA CLYTTE - KEMMEL Barrier at 8.30 p.m.

Machine Gunners & Limbers will march off from bivouacs at 7.40 p.m. and will be met by guides at Bn. H.Q. RIGHT SECTOR.

Signallers will report at H.Q. RIGHT SECTOR at 2.30 p.m. and take over telephones.

O.C. 1st. Bn. York & Lancaster Regt. will command Right Sector until reliefs are complete.

Completion of reliefs will be reported to Bn. H.Q. by telephone.

Trench garrisons will be told off before leaving bivouacs at SCHERPENBERG.

Distribution, Situation, and Ammunition Expenditure Reports will be rendered to Bn. H.Q. at 4 a.m. tomorrow.

1 Coy. 6th. Bn. Leicestershire Regt. will be attached to the Battn. for a tour of 48 hours in the trenches.

This Coy. will be attached as follows :-

1 Platoon to A Coy. 1 Platoon to B Coy. 1 Platoon to D Coy.

1 Platoon will be in the trenches occupied by the 2 Coys. of 5th. Bn. The King's Own Regt. (H. Trenches).

2 Coys. & 2 M.Gs. 5th. Bn. The King's Own Regt. now in the Trenches will come under the Orders of the O.C. 2nd. Bn. The King's Own Regt. on completion of reliefs.

J.F.B. Morrell

Captain,
Adjutant, 2nd. Bn. The King's Own Regiment.

Officers' Kits.

Officers' Kits will be collected at 5.30 p.m.

Blankets.

Blankets will be rolled in bundles of ten, and handed over to Sergt. Memory who will be at the entrance to the field near H.Q. camp at 3 p.m.

Bivouacs.

Bivouacs will be left standing & the lines will be thoroughly cleaned before they are vacated.

App. 2.

S E C R E T

COPY No. 2

OPERATION ORDER No. 59.

by

BRIGADIER GENERAL H.S.L.Ravenshaw C.M.G.

Commanding 83rd Infantry Brigade

Reference VIERSTRAAT 1/10,000 and Sheet 28 1/40,000

10th August 1915.

1. (a) On night 11th - 12th August 2/King's Own Regt. will relieve 1/York & Lancaster Regt. in the Right Sector.

(b) The two companies and two machine guns 5/King's Own R. now attached to 1/York & Lancaster Regt. will come under the orders of O.C. 2/King's Own Regt. on completion of relief.

(c) All details of relief will be arranged between Officers Comdg. 2/King's Own Regt. and 1/York & Lancaster Regt. necessary reconnaissance will be carried out before relief. Relieving units will not pass barrier on LA CLYTTE - KEMMEL road before 8.15 p.m.

(d) Signallers of relieving units will take over at 3 p.m. 11th instant.

(e) O.C. 1/York & Lancaster Regt. will command in Right Sector until relief is completed. Completion of relief to be wired to this office.

2. On relief 1/York & Lancaster Regt. will take over bivouacs at SCHERPENBERG vacated by 2/King's Own Regt.

3. At 2 p.m. 11th August 5/King's Own Regt. will move to bivouac in square , M.11.c.4.5. with their transport in M.17.c.6.5.

4. At 4 p.m. 11August the 3/Monmouth Regt. join the Brigade and will bivouac in square M.22.d.4.6 with their transport in square M.22.c.9.6. These fields are now occupied by 5/King's Own Regt.

Issued at 4-45 p.m.

R.S. Follett Captain
Brigade Major
83rd Infantry Brigade

Copy No.1. War Diary
2. 2/King's Own
3. 2/East Yorks
4. 1/K.O.Y.L.I.
5. 1/York & Lancs.
6. 5/King's Own.
7. 3/Monmouths.
8. 28th Divn.
9. 84th Brigade.
10. 3rd Brigade R.F.A.
11. No 2 Coy A.S.C.
12. O.C.Signals 83rd Bde.
13. M.G.O.83rd Brigade.

App. 4.

SECRET. COPY No. 2

OPERATION ORDER No. 61

by

Brigadier-General H.S.L.Ravenshaw, C.M.G.,

Commanding 83rd Infantry Brigade.

****

Reference VIERSTRAAT 1/10.000 and Sheet 28 1/40,000

Thursday, 12th August, 1915.

1. The two Companies 6th Leicester Regiment, now attached 2nd King's Own Regiment and 2nd East Yorks will be withdrawn from the trenches tonight, and will rejoin their Battalion Headquarters.

2\. a. On night 13th-14th August, the 6th Leicester Regiment will be distributed in trenches as follows :-

Attached to 2nd King's Own:-

Senior Major,
Medical Officer
Half stretcher bearers.
Half Signallers,
Half machine gunners,
Two Companies.

Attached to 1st K.O.Y.L.I. :-

Commanding Officer.
Adjutant,
Half Stretcher bearers.
Half Signallers,
Half Machine Gunners,
Two Companies.

b. Guides will be furnished by both Sector Commanders at the barrier on LA CLYTTE - KEMMEL road N.20.b.8.8., at 8.15.p M., to meet 6th Leicester Regiment.

c. The above Companies will garrison fire and support trenches. Machine gunners, signallers and stretcher bearers will be attached to corresponding branch of 2nd King's Own and 1st K.O.Y.L.I. 6th Leicester Regiment will not bring their own machine guns.

3. On night 13th-14th, after arrival of 6th Leicester Regt.

a. The two Companies 5th King's Own Regiment attached to 2nd King's Own Regiment will rejoin the Headquarters of their own Battalion.

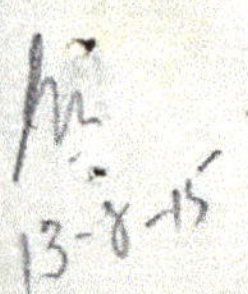

b. One Company 1st K.O.Y.L.I., will proceed to bivouacs at SCHERPENBERG.

4. On night 15th - 16th August :-

a. Two Companies 5th King's Own Regiment will relieve two Companies 6th Leicester Regiment attached to 2nd King's Own Regiment.

b. One Company 1st K.O.Y.L.I., from SCHERPENBERG will rejoin 1st K.O.Y.L.I., when the two Companies 6th Leicester Regiment attached to 1st K.O.Y.L.I., will be withdrawn.

c. On completion of relief and move, 6th Leicester Regiment will return to LOCREHOF FARM.

5. All details regarding reliefs and moves will be arranged between Officers Commanding 2nd King's Own Regiment and 1st K.O.Y.L.I., and Officer Commanding 6th Leicester Regiment.

6. Completion of reliefs will be wired to Brigade Headquarters

R.S. Follett Captain.

Issued at 10 p.m. Brigade Major. 83rd Brigade.

Copy No. 1, War Diary.
2, 2nd King's Own.Regt.
3, 2nd East Yorkshire Regt.
4, 1st K.O.Y.L.I.
5, 1st York & Lancaster Regt.
6, 5th King's Own Regt.
7, 3rd Monmouth Regt.
8, 6th Leicester Regt.
9, 110th Brigade.
10, 28th Division.
11, 3rd Brigade R.F.A.
12, No. 2 Coy A.S.C.
13, Signals, 83rd Brigade.
14, Machine Gun Officer, 83rd Brigade.

app. 5.

S E C R E T. Copy No...2....

OPERATION ORDER No.62.

by

BRIGADIER GENERAL H.S.L.Ravenshaw C.M.G.

Commanding 83rd Infantry Brigade.

Reference, VIERSTRAAT 1/10,000
Sheet 28 1/40,000

16th August 1915.

1. (a) On night 17th - 18th August 1/York & Lancaster Regt., will relieve 2/King's Own Regt., in the present Right Sector, 5/King's Own garrison in H.5 & their Machine Gun team in S.P.12..

(b) 5/King's Own Regt., will hand over their Machine Gun in S.P.12 to 1/York & Lancs., and will leave 25 men in H.5, who will come under orders of 1/York & Lancaster Regt..

2. (a) On night 17th - 18th August 5/King's Own Regt. will take over from Northumberland Fusiliers 84th Brigade the following trenches:-

G.4	35 men
G.4.a	50 men
New Sap	65 men & 1 Machine Gun.
H.1	55 men
S.P.11	30 men & 1 Machine Gun,

and will still garrison trenches H.2 & H.3, the command of which will pass to O.C. 5/King's Own with 25 men in H.5 as in para 1.(b).

(b) Headquarters 5/King's Own Regt., will be at the Stables KEMMEL CHATEAU.

3. (a) All details of reliefs will be arranged between the Commanding Officers of battalions concerned.

(b) Signallers of relieving units will take over at 3 p.m. 17th instant.

(c) Relieving units will pass barrier N.20.b.6.8
5/King's Own Regt at 8 p.m.
1/York & Lancaster Regt at 8.15 p.m.

(d) On relief 2/King's Own Regt. move to bivouacs SCHERPENBERG

4. Lists of trench stores taken over from Northumberland Fus. will be sent to this office.

5. Completion of reliefs will be wired to this office.

6. On completion of relief 83rd Brigade front will be divided into three sectors:-

Right Sector	5/King's Own Regt.
Centre Sector	1/York & Lancaster Regt.
Left Sector	1/K.O.Y.L.I.

Issued at 10 p.m.

R.S. Follett Captain
Brigade Major
83rd Infantry Brigade.

Copy No.1 War Diary
2 2/King's Own
3 2/East Yorks
4 1/K.O.Y.L.I.
5 1/York & Lancs.
6 5/King's Own
7 3/Monmouths
8 28th Divn.
9 84th Brigade
10 3rd Bde R.F.A.
11 No.2 Coy A.S.C.
12 Staff Captain
13 O.C. Signals 83rd Bde.
14 M.G.O. 83rd Bde.

J.B. 17/8/15

OPERATION ORDERS No. 28.

by

Lieut. Col. E.M. Morris
Comdg 2/Bn. The King's Own Regt.

App. 5.

ROSSIGNOL
17/8/15.

Relief 1. The Battalion will be relieved in the Trenches tonight by 1st Bn. York & Lancaster Regt.

Reports 2. Reliefs Complete will be reported by Telephone to Battn. Head Quarters.

Command 3. Lieut. Col. E.M. Morris will be in Command until relief is complete.

Companies 4. On relief being reported Complete Companies will march back independantly to the Bivouacs at SCHERPENBERG.

Signallers 5. The Signallers of 1st York & Lancaster Regt. will take over Telephones by 3 pm.

Officers 6. Officers of relieving Unit will take over Trench Stores early this evening.

Returns 7. Handing over statements of Trench Stores will be handed in to Orderly room by 10. am tomorrow.

1 Co

J.F.B. Morrell Capt. & Adjt.
2 The King's Own Regt.

App 6.

S E C R E T. Copy No....2...

OPERATION ORDER No. 65.

by

BRIGADIER GENERAL H.S.L.Ravenshaw C.M.G.

Commanding 83rd Infantry Brigade.

Reference, VIERSTRAAT 1/10,000
Sheet 28 1/40,000

22nd August 1915.

1. (a) On the night 23rd - 24th August 2/King's Own Regt., will relieve 1/York & Lancaster Regt., in Centre Sector.

(b) The twenty five men of 3/Monmouth Regt., in H.5 will come under the orders of O.C. 2/King's Own Regt., on completion of relief.

2. On night 24th - 25th August 1/K.O.Y.L.I. will relieve 2/East Yorkshire Regt., in Left Sector.

3. (a) All details of above reliefs will be arranged between Commanding Officers concerned.

(b) Relieving units will pass barrier N.20.b.6.8 at 7.45 p.m.

(c) Signallers of relieving units will take over at 3 p.m. on the day of relief.

(d) Commanding Officers of Battalions to be relieved will command in their sectors until relief is completed. Completion of relief to be wired to this office.

Issued at 7.45 p.m.

R.S. Follett
Captain
Brigade Major
83rd Infantry Brigade.

Copy No.1 War Diary
2 2/King's Own
3 2/East Yorks
4 1/K.O.Y.L.I.
5 1/York & Lancs
6 5/King's Own
7 3/Monmouths
8 28th Division
9 84th Brigade
10 3rd Bde R.F.A.
11 2/1 Northumbrian Fd.Co.R.E.
12 No.2 Coy.A.S.C.
13 O.C. Signals 83rd Bde
14 M.G.Officer 83rd Bde
15 Staff Captain.

Km.
22/8/15

App. 6 60

OPERATION ORDERS NO. 29.
By Lieut. Colonel E.M. Morris,
Commdg. 2nd. Bn. The King's Own Regiment.

MONDAY. 23.8.1915.

- -

The Battalion will relieve the 1st. Bn. York & Lancs. Regt. in the trenches of the CENTRE SECTOR on the night 23rd/24th. August 1915 (tonight).

Coys. will march off in the following order at three minutes interval :-

Machine Gunners	-	6.40 p.m.
C Company	...	6.43 p.m.
A "	...	6.46 p.m.
B Coy.	...	6.49 p.m.
D Coy.	...	6.52 p.m.
H.Qrs.	...	6.55 p.m.

Signallers will take over telephones at 3 p.m. this afternoon.

O.C. C Coy. will detail 36 men and O.C. D Coy. will detail 14 men - - - This party will form the garrison of trench H.5. under command of Lieut. G.L. Chesney. This party will march off in rear of B Coy. (6.49 p.m.).

25 men of the 3rd. Bn. Mons. Regt. in H.5. will come under command of O.C. 2nd. Bn. The King's Own Regt. on completion of relief.

Commanding Officers of Battalions to be relieved will command in their Sectors until reliefs are completed.

Completion of reliefs will be reported to Bn. H.Q. by telephone.

Situation, Distribution, Ammunition Expenditure Reports and Indents for trench Stores, will be rendered to Bn. H.Q. by 4 a.m. tomorrow.

J.B. Mowell
Captain,
Adjutant, 2nd. Bn. The King's Own Regiment.

OFFICERS KITS.

Officers kits will be collected at 5 p.m.

BLANKETS.

Blankets will be rolled in bundles of ten, and handed over to Sergt. Memory who will be at the entrance to the field near H.Q. camp at 3 p.m.

BIVOUACS.

Bivouacs will be left standing and the lines will be thoroughly cleaned before they are vacated.

S E C R E T.

Copy No..2......

OPERATION ORDER No. 66.

by

BRIGADIER GENERAL H.S.L.Ravenshaw C.M.G.

Commanding 83rd Infantry Brigade.

app 7

Reference, VIERSTRAAT 1/10,000
Sheet 28 1/40,000

27th August 1915.

1. On night 28th - 29th August 5/King's Own Regt will relieve 3/Monmouth Regt in Right Sector and the Machine Gun teams 2/King's Own Regt & 1/K.O.Y.L.I.

2. On night 29th - 30th August 1/York & Lancaster Regt will relieve 2/King's Own Regt in centre sector.

3. On night 30th - 31st August 2/East Yorkshire Regt will relieve 1/K.O.Y.L.I. in Left Sector.

4.(a) All details of above relief will be arranged between Commanding Officers concerned.

(b) Relieving units will pass the barrier N.20.b.6.8 at 7.15 p.m.

(c) Signallers of reliving units will take over at 3 p.m. on day of relief.

5.(a) Officers Commanding battalions to be relieved will command in their sectors until the relief is completed.

(b) Completion of relief to be wired to this office.

Issued at 9.35a.m.

[signature]
Captain
Brigade Major
83rd Infantry Brigade.

Copy No.1 War Diary.
2 2/King's Own
3 2/East Yorks
4 1/K.O.Y.L.I.
5 1/York & Lancs
6 5/King's Own
7 3/Monmouths
8 28th Division
9 84th Brigade
10 3rd Bde R.F.A.
11 No.2 Coy.A.S.C.
12 2/1 Northumbrian Fd.Co.R.E.
13 O.C.Signals 83rd Bde.
14 M.G.Officer 83rd Bde
15 Staff Captain.

OPERATION ORDERS No 30.

by

Lieut Col. E M Morris

Comd 7/Bn [illegible] [illegible] Inf

App 7.

ROSSIGNOL
29/8/15

Relief 1. The Battalion will be relieved in the trenches of Centre Section by 1st Bn [illegible] Lancashire Regt on Night of 29th/30th August.

Telephones 2. Signallers of relieving units will take over Telephones at 3 pm.

3. The relief companies and M. Gns will march back independently to the same [illegible] at SCHERPENBERG as when last at rest.

Reports 4. The following reports will be rendered
(a) Handing over and taking over reports will be rendered to Bn. H.Q. by 5 pm.
(b) Duplicate list of Trench Stores will be handed in to orderly room by 10 am tomorrow
(c) Work done reports for work carried out during the day will be telephoned to Bn. H.Q. by 8 pm this evening.

Command 5 Officers Commanding Battalions to be relieved will command in their Sectors until relief is complete.

Completion of Relief .6. Reliefs complete will be reported to Bn. H. Qrs.

J F B Russell Capt & Adjt
[illegible]

83rd Bde.

28th Division.

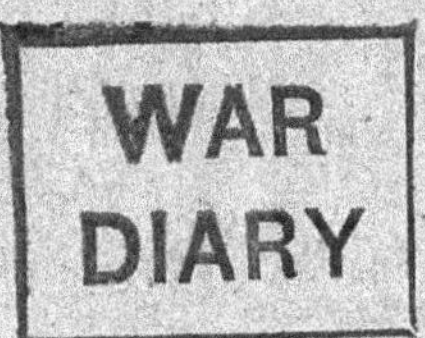

2nd KING'S OWN ROYAL LANCS.

S E P T E M B E R

1 9 1 5

Instructions regarding War Diaries and Intelligence Summaries are contained in F. S. Regs., Part II. and the Staff Manual respectively. Title Pages will be prepared in manuscript.

WAR DIARY
or
INTELLIGENCE SUMMARY
(Erase heading not required.)

Army Form C. 2118

Place	Date	Hour	Summary of Events and Information	Remarks and references to Appendices
SCHERPENBERG	Sept 1st		Battalion at Rest. 700 men out working on Subsidiary Line during day & night.	
"	Sept 2nd-3rd		" " " 150 men out working on Subsidiary Line during the night of Sept 3rd.	
"	Sept 4th	7.30pm	Battalion relieved 1st Bn York & Lancaster Regt in the Trenches of Right Sector (H2-K1a with S.P.12 & 13) Detachment of 2 Coys 5th King's Own Came under command of O.C. Battn. These two Companies Garrison G.4-H1 inclusive. Reinforcements. Two Officers (2nd Lts Stonnell & Cole from Cadet School St Omer) & 17 Other Ranks.	
KEMMELL	Sept 5th-8th		Battalion in the Trenches. The enemy's artillery shelled the ground intermittently each day without doing any damage they also Whizz Banged and shelled our trenches K.1.a & S.P.13 in the evening of 8th. Our Artillery were fairly active each day dropping shrapnel into PETIT BOIS opposite our trenches. Casualties during this period O.R. Killed 1 Wounded 3. Col: Morris having taken over Command of the Brigade on 5th Capt & Adjt J.F.B. Morrell Commanded the Battalion	
"	Sept 9th	10.30am	Battalion in the Trenches. The enemy threw Rifle grenades into J.1. Trench, but we replied with Artillery Trench Mortars & bombs; & at 11.30 Am all was quiet.	
		11. am.	The enemy fired trench mortars into K.1. Our Trench Mortars replied also our Artillery & by 12.15 pm the enemy were silenced. Very little damage was done to trenches in above attacks.	
		7.50pm	A Bore hole was exploded by the Brigade mining section in the left of J.3 Right in order to stop the enemy's mining which had been heard close to this Trench. No damage done to Galleries, but the left end of J.3 Right was blown down by the explosion & was built up again. J.1 & J.3 Left opened fire.	
		8. pm	The enemy opened fire with trench mortars into K.1 J.3. New, & J.4. Our Trench Mortars & Artillery replied silencing the enemy by 9.30pm. Casualties O.R. wounded 4	
"	Sept 10th		Battalion in the trenches. The enemy's Aeroplanes have been very active for the last three days flying over our lines; and apparently spotting for their Artillery which have shelled us intermittently. The Battalion was relieved in the trenches at 9.15 pm by 1st Bn. York & Lancaster Regt	[illegible signature]

1875 Wt. W593/826 1,000,000 4/15 J.B.C. & A. A.D.S.S./Forms/C. 2118.

Instructions regarding War Diaries and Intelligence Summaries are contained in F. S. Regs., Part II. and the Staff Manual respectively. Title Pages will be prepared in manuscript.

WAR DIARY
or
INTELLIGENCE SUMMARY
(Erase heading not required.)

Army Form C. 2118

Place	Date	Hour	Summary of Events and Information	Remarks and references to Appendices
KEMMEL	Sept 10th		On Relief the Battalion proceeded to Billets at LOCRE which we previously occupied in June.	
LOCRE	Sept 11th–16th		Battalion at rest in Billets at LOCRE. Casualties during this period O.R wounded 2.	
"	Sept 16th	6.45pm	The Battalion relieved the 7th Battn York & Lancashire Regt in the Right Sector in front of KEMMEL. occupying the same Trenches as last Tour.	
KEMMEL	Sept 17th		The Battalion in the trenches. The enemy fired about 20 H.E 5.9" shells at K3 Trench at 12.45 pm doing a certain amount of damage to trench & particularly the M.G emplacement. Our Heavy Artillery retaliated. Casualties up to Midday Nil. Our Aeroplanes observed our Artillery fire reported damage to enemy's trenches in PETIT BOIS	
" "	Sept 18th	4.30pm	The Battalion in the trenches. The enemy dropped 6 8" H.E shells behind G.4a Trench in retaliation to our Artillery which had been very active all the morning. Casualties up to midday O.R. Wounded 2 one at duty.	
" "	Sept 19th	11.15am 2 pm 5 pm 7 pm	The enemy shelled K.11 with 5.9" shells at the same time we fired trench mortars from 51 & H.a. in retaliation silencing the enemy. The enemy again bombarded K1 Trench at 2 pm & at 5 pm this last time with heavy trench mortars & a good deal of damage was done to parapet and Communication Trench. On all occasions our Artillery replied, silencing the enemy.	
" "	Sept 20th	7.30pm	15 officers of 25th Canadian Regt of 5th Canadian Brigade reconnoitred the Trenches of Right Sector and two Platoons from each Company of 21st Canadian Regt took over trenches of the Right Sector relieving the whole of D Coy. "C" Company was relieved by 1 Platoon 22nd Canadian Regt. Casualties Nil	
" "	Sept 21st		½ The Battn & ½ Battn 25th Canadians holding trenches of Right Sector.	
" "	Sept 22nd	8.45pm	The remaining ½ of the Battn in Right Sector relieved by the remaining two Platoons of each Company of 25th Canadian Regt & 2 Platoons 22nd Canadian Regt also the M.G.s in Right Sector relieved by M.Gs 5th Canadian Brigade. The whole Battalion ~~[illegible]~~ bivouacing for the night at LOCRE.	
CLAPBANK	Sept 23rd	9 am	The Battalion moved from bivouacs LOCRE to BILLETS at CLAPBANK, the same ones as occupied by the Battalion in January. The Brigade is billetted in the area OUTTERSTEEN – CLAPBANK. The 25th Division now forms the Army Reserve to Second Army	
"	Sept 24th & 25th		Battalion in Billets. Route marches & training are being carried out	

1875 Wt. W593/826 1,000,000 4/15 J.B.C. & A. A.D.S.S./Forms/C. 2118.

Instructions regarding War Diaries and Intelligence Summaries are contained in F. S. Regs., Part II. and the Staff Manual respectively. Title pages will be prepared in manuscript.

WAR DIARY
or
INTELLIGENCE SUMMARY.
(Erase heading not required.)

Army Form C. 2118.

Place	Date	Hour	Summary of Events and Information	Remarks and references to Appendices
CLAPBANK	Sept 26	5 am	The Battalion moved by march Route with the Brigade to MERVILLE on arrival there we were ordered to continue our march to ROBECQ where we arrived at 12 noon. At 2 pm we continued our march towards BETHUNE but when about two miles EAST of ROBECQ we were ordered to return to our BILLETS at ROBECQ, where we remained for the night	
ROBECQ	Sept 27	12 noon	The Battalion moved with the Brigade by Buses to BETHUNE thence to NOYELLES where we bivouaced in a field Battalion H Q being in an "Estaminet". The Battalion & 7th K.O.Y.L.I. were now Reserve to the 83rd Brigade.	
NOYELLES	Sept 28		The Battalion remained at NOYELLES weather wet.	
NOYELLES	" 29	11 am	The Battalion with 1st K.O.Y.L.I. were moved up through VERMELLES into the LANCASHIRE TRENCH North East of this place and Company Comdrs went up to the first line in the Old German Trenches to reconnoitre them as we were ordered to Relief the Worcesters & 60th Rifles in the old German Trenches known as the QUARRY TRENCH North of the VERMELLES-HULLOCH Road from BRESLAU trench on the Right to St ELIE AVENUE on the Left both these avenues being old German C Ts. The Camerons & Wilts were on our Right, the East Yorks on our Left.	
QUARRY TRENCH	" 30		The Battalion remained in the trenches & much work was done to improve them. Except for a bomb attack by the Germans on our Left in St ELIE AVENUE the Situation was normal. The Camerons on our Right were relieved by 1st K.O.Y.L.I.	

D. D. & L., London, E.C.
(A0349) Wt W3900/P713 750,000 3/18 E 2688 Forms C/2118/16.

83rd Bde.
28th Div.

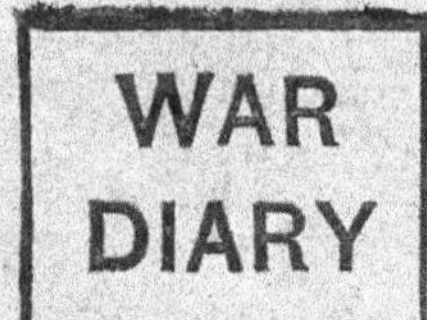

WAR DIARY

Embarked with Division for Salonøka 1.11.15.

2nd K. O. R. LANCS.

OCTOBER

1 9 1 5

Instructions regarding War Diaries and Intelligence Summaries are contained in F. S. Regs., Part II. and the Staff Manual respectively. Title pages will be prepared in manuscript.

WAR DIARY
or
INTELLIGENCE SUMMARY.
(Erase heading not required.)

Army Form C. 2118.

Place	Date	Hour	Summary of Events and Information	Remarks and references to Appendices
"	Oct 1st	10 pm	The Battalion was relieved by 60th Rifles, the whole of 83rd Brigade being relieved from the trenches by a Brigade of 6th Division. The Relief was complete at 1.10 AM Oct 2nd & the Battalion moved back to billets at ANNEQUIN West of VERMELLES.	
			Casualties from Sept 29th – Oct 2nd Officers wounded 1 (2nd Lieut Moore-Williams) Other Ranks Killed 9 wounded 38 missing 1.	
ANNEQUIN	Oct 2nd		The Battalion remained in Billets.	
	Oct 3rd	5.0 AM	The Battalion was ordered to move at once to support 84th Brigade & moved off at 6.5 am to CLARKS KEEP where	B.M.B 83
		8 am	we received orders that we should still remain under the orders of 83rd Brigade & were to move to LANCASHIRE TRENCH	C.1.346
		11 am	we received orders to relieve Northumberland Fusiliers in BIG WILLIE & at 12 noon the Battalion moved up via	BM.677
		5.45 pm	CTs HULLOCH ALLEY – STANSFIELD ROAD – SPURN HEAD SAP to relieve, the relief was complete at 5.45 pm	
			D Coy were left at LANCASHIRE TRENCH & attached to 1st K.O.Y.L.I. as a Reserve Company.	
		7.15 pm	Col. MORRIS reported the situation	K.O.3 [illegible]

1875 Wt. W593/826 1,000,000 4/15 J.B.C. & A. A.D.S.S./Forms/C. 2118.

D. D. & L., London, E.C.
(10340) Wt W5300/P713 750,000 3/18 E 2688 Forms C/2118/18.

Army Form C. 2118

Instructions regarding War Diaries and Intelligence Summaries are contained in F. S. Regs., Part II. and the Staff Manual respectively. Title Pages will be prepared in manuscript.

WAR DIARY
or
INTELLIGENCE SUMMARY
(Erase heading not required.)

Place	Date	Hour	Summary of Events and Information	Remarks and references to Appendices
BIG WILLIE	OCT 3rd	10.25 pm	Except for intermittent Bombing by the enemy who occupied a portion of BIG WILLIE from about 50x South of POINT 60, which was retaken by them the previous evening, and the enemy who occupied their original front line about 60x North of the WINDOW the situation was normal although we were fired at from front & flank (left) by Rifle fire & M.G.s. (The C.O. now sent off his second report)	K.O. 4 attd.
"	Oct. 4th	1.15	The Commanding Officer received the following order from G.O.C. 83rd Brigade "Endeavour to Capture POINT 60 at end of BIG WILLIE before Dawn. AAA Am ATTACKING Redoubt at dawn AAA Acknowledge". (The redoubt referred to was the HOENZOLLERN Redoubt to the North of BIG WILLIE retaken by the enemy on Evening of Oct 2nd). This was acknowledged at 1.20 AM. and the C.O. issued his orders to A Coy for the attack with bombs	B.M. 636 attd. K.O. 6 K.O. 7
"	"	9 am	The Brigade received a report on the situation & what progress had been made. The C.O. replied with a report both to the Brigade and Division	B.M. 646 attd.
"	"	1 pm	The C.O. received a memorandum from Brigadier General Rawlinson Comdg 83rd Brigade asking for a report regarding our position & situation in BIG WILLIE	K.O. 7 & 8 attd. B.M. 648 attd.
			The C.O. replied to the above at 3.15 pm	K.O. 12 attd.
			Much work in improving the trench was carried on & wire & Sandbags were called for urgently. The day passed quietly except for rifle & MG fire & occasional Whiz bangs.	
"	Oct 5th	2 am	The enemy pushed a strong bomb attack on our right which lasted about 3/4 of an hour. A report is attached. At the same time a small bomb attack was launched against our left which was easily repulsed.	K.O. 21 attd.
			The weather was very bad all day and the enemy fired several MINNINGWERFER into the trench during the morning.	K.O. 24 attd.
		12 noon	The C.O. & Coy Comdrs of 3rd Grenadier Guards came up to reconnoitre the trenches as they are relieving the Battalion at night.	
	Oct 6th	4.15 am	The relief was very late arriving (1.15 am) and the relief was not complete until 4.15 am when Companies marched back independently to billets at ANNEQUIN the last company arriving about 8 am.	
ANNEQUIN		~~2 pm~~	The total casualties for the tour in BIG WILLIE were Officers wounded two (2nd Lieut Ballard & 2nd Lieut Milner, the latter only slightly and at duty) OR Killed 4 wounded 35, missing 1. Officers evacuated sick 3 (Lieut Sommerville, & 2nd Lieuts Tucker & Markland).	
"		2.30 pm	The Battalion moved with the Brigade to GONNEHEM via BETHUNE [illegible]	
		6.30 pm	The Battalion arrived at GONNEHEM	

Army Form C. 2118

WAR DIARY
or
INTELLIGENCE SUMMARY
(Erase heading not required.)

Instructions regarding War Diaries and Intelligence Summaries are contained in F. S. Regs., Part II. and the Staff Manual respectively. Title Pages will be prepared in manuscript.

Place	Date	Hour	Summary of Events and Information	Remarks and references to Appendices
GONNEHEM	Oct 7th		Bn in billets with remainder 83rd Bde.	
	Oct 9th		2 Lieut Peers accidentally wounded while standing 50x from some men practicing with bombs in the opposite direction.	
	Oct 13th		The battalion paraded with the Brigade for inspection by the new G.O.C. 28th Div (Gen Briggs)	
	Oct 15th	4.3 pm	The Bn with the remainder of the Brigade marched into billets at LA PREOL. Lt GODDING RAMC to hospital Capt LAWTON RAMC acting M.O.	
LA PREOL	Oct 16th		The C.O. Coy Cmdrs & M.G.O. make a reconnaissance of 22nd Bde Trenches in the vicinity of CAMBRIN. 2 Lt CURSHAM reported his arrival and was posted to A Coy. 2 Lt O'BRIEN evacuated sick.	
CUINCHY	Oct 18th		The battalion marched from LA PREOL and took over Trenches from R. Welch Fusiliers Bn. H.Q being at CUINCHY CHATEAU	
	Oct 21st		The Bn was relieved at about 11.45 am by the 2/S. Staffordshire Rgt. The tour was on a whole without any remarkable occurrence. On 19th the enemy did considerable damage to our Left Front Trench destroying about 50x of parapet killing 4 other ranks and wounding or injuring by burying 6 other ranks. Our artillery retaliated effectually. The Bn held from the bank of the canal to HANOVER ST. Distribution 2 Coys in Firing Line C and B, D Coy in support and A Coy in reserve. Total casualties 5 killed and 14 wounded (O.R.)	
GONNEHEM	Oct 21st		The Bn marched to billets for the night at GONNEHEM arriving at about 6 pm.	
	Oct 22nd	10.35 pm	The Bn marched from GONNEHEM to FOUQUEREUIL where it entrained at 10.35 pm. 2/Lts KNOX, BEDFORD, [struck-through word] LLOYD 5th The King's Own & 2 Lt HAROLD & MONKS 10/N Staffs joined the Bn for duty.	
MARSEILLES	October 26th 10.30am	10.30am	The Bn arrived at MARSEILLES (GARE DE CHARLES) at 6.30 am after unloading train marched through town headed by the Brigade to the Docks, the populace giving it a great ovation. At the Docks the Bn embarked on the HT ALNWICK CASTLE only Hdqr and 5 Coy Cmdrs were accommodated the remainder of officers on S.S. KYARRA. Transport and wagons loaded, but horses and men left at MARSEILLES under Capt M.C. PEAKE.	W. J. [illegible] Capt & Adjt. October 26th 1915

Instructions regarding War Diaries and Intelligence Summaries are contained in F. S. Regs., Part II. and the Staff Manual respectively. Title pages will be prepared in manuscript.

Army Form C. 2118.

WAR DIARY
or
INTELLIGENCE SUMMARY.
(Erase heading not required.)

Place	Date	Hour	Summary of Events and Information	Remarks and references to Appendices
S.S. ALNWICK CASTLE	26/10/15	6 am	The ALNWICK CASTLE sailed for ALEXANDRIA with Battalion on board & 2 Companies of 2 East Yorkshire Rgt. Total 1036 all ranks.	
"	27th-30th Oct:		On Board ALNWICK CASTLE	
"	Oct: 31st	9.30 am	On board. Submarine sighted about 6 miles behind us; which chased us for ½ an hour and then dived. Troops went to Boat stations & remained there until 1 pm. A wireless message was sent out at 10.30 am that we had been chased and that a Submarine was in the vicinity, with the result that a French Destroyer came up to us, but went away shortly after we had spoken to her.	

D. D. & L., London, E.C.
(10340) Wt W5300/P713 750,000 3/18 E 2688 Forms C/2118/15.

"A" Form. Army Form C

MESSAGES AND SIGNALS. No. of Message

…Code … m.	Words	Charge	This message is on a/c of:	Recd. at
…f Origin and Service Instructions.	Sent		……Service.	Date
Secret.	At … m.			From
	To			By
	By		(Signature of "Franking Officer.")	

TO: a/Kings Own ~~[illegible]~~ / ~~1/K.O.Y.L.I.~~ ~~[illegible]~~

Sender's Number.	Day of Month	In reply to Number	
*BMB 53	2		AAA

83rd Bde relieve 84th Bde on night 3rd 4th inst ~~AAA~~ reconnoitring officers will be prepared to leave billets 11 am the 3rd inst these officers will await the arrival of their battalions at BARTS. on completion of reconnaissance operation orders will be issued in the morning.

From 83rd Bde

Place

Time 10.20 PM

The above may be forwarded as now corrected. (Z) R. S. Follett Major

Censor. Signature of Addressor or person authorised to telegraph in his name.

* This line should be erased if not required.

(771-5) —McC. & Co. Ltd., London.— W 1739/1402. 150,000. 8/15. Forms C 2121/10.

"A" Form. Army Form C. 2121.

MESSAGES AND SIGNALS.

No. of Message ....

Prefix .... Code .... m. | Words | Charge

Office of Origin and Service Instructions.

This message is on a/c of: .... Service.

Sent At .... m. To .... By ....

(Signature of "Franking Officer.")

Recd. at .... m. Date .... From .... By ....

[Stamp: YB 3 X 15 HR — TELEGRAPHS]

TO Second Kings Own ~~83rd~~ Infy Bde ~~84th~~

Sender's Number.	Day of Month	In reply to Number	AAA
* G.1. 346	Third		

Do not move up to 84th Bde HQ but take ~~position about~~ in LANCASHIRE TRENCH ~~about~~ and SUSSEX TRENCH west and north of BARTS AAA You will ~~respectively~~ remain ~~under orders~~ 83rd Bde ~~Orders~~ AAA. Addressed Second Kings Own repeated 83rd and 84th Infy Bdes

From 28th Div

Place

Time 7 am

The above may be forwarded as now corrected. (Z) Y. R. Schuster Major G.S.

Censor. Signature of Addressor or person authorised to telegraph in his name.

* This line should be erased if not required.

9) —McC. & Co. Ltd., London.— W 14142/641. 225,000 4/15. Forms C2121/10.

"A" Form.

Army Form

MESSAGES AND SIGNALS.

No. of Message

Prefix ..... Code ..... m.	Words	Charge	This message is on a/c of:	Recd. at
Office of Origin and Service Instructions.	Sent		..... Service.	Date
Priority	At ..... m.			From
	To			
	By		(Signature of "Franking Officer.")	By

TO 2/Kings Own Regt

Sender's Number.	Day of Month	In reply to Number	
* BM 627	third		AAA

Your Battalion will move at once via VERMELLES and BARTS down CENTRAL TRENCH to CENTRAL KEEP G 3 d 4 5 AAA On arrival at CENTRAL TRENCH you will come under orders of GOC 84th Bde AAA at CLARKS KEEP a guide from 84th Bde will meet and conduct Battalion to CENTRAL KEEP AAA This move will not affect the position in the line you will hold tonight AAA Acknowledge and report [illegible] you move off.

From 83rd Brigade

Place

Time 4–40 AM

The above may be forwarded as now corrected.

Censor.

(Z) R S Follett Major

Signature of Addressor or person authorised to telegraph in his name.

* This line should be erased if not required.

-5) —McC. & Co. Ltd., London.— W 1789/1402. 150,000 8/15. Forms C 2121/10.

"A" Form.

Army Form C. 2121.

MESSAGES AND SIGNALS.

No. of Message

Prefix Code m. | Words | Charge | This message is on a/c of: | Recd. at m.

Office of Origin and Service Instructions.

Sent At m. To By

Service.

(Signature of "Franking Officer.")

Date From By

TO 83w Brigade

Sender's Number. KO 3 | Day of Month 3/10/15 | In reply to Number | AAA

Am holding trench BIG WILLIE from near the WINDOW to my right as far as just short of Point 60 South West of South face AAA There is no communication to support trenches except by SPURN HEAD AAA a C.T. should be constructed if possible from my line back AAA Can this be done by reserve Companies AAA I cannot undertake this owing to the situation which is not yet very clear AAA I must also ask you to send me my rations

From and water which I believe are dumped at

Place BARTS AAA. I have no sandbags and

Time

The above may be forwarded as now corrected.

(Z)

Censor.

Signature of Addressor or person authorised to telegraph in his name.

* This line should be erased if not required.

(632) —McC. & Co. Ltd., London.— W 11400/2045. 100,000. 2/15. Forms C 2121/10.

"A" Form. Army Form C. 2121.

MESSAGES AND SIGNALS.

No. of Message

Prefix ... Code ... m.	Words	Charge	This message is on a/c of:	Recd. at ... m.
Office of Origin and Service Instructions.	Sent		... Service.	Date
	At ... m.			From
	To			
	By		(Signature of "Franking Officer.")	By

TO

Sender's Number.	Day of Month	In reply to Number	AAA
*			

Can	do	with	as	many
as	you	can	send	me
AAA	They	are	urgently	needed
AAA	I	have	plenty	of
bombs	for	tonight	but	think
a	supply	spare	be	sent
up	daily	AAA	Could	not
a	Staff	officer	be	sent
me	in	order	that	situation
here	may	be	brought	back
to	you	verbally	?	Consider
this	important	AAA.		

J B Russell Capt & Adjt

From O.C. Kings Own

Place

Time 7.15 pm

The above may be forwarded as now corrected.

Censor.

(Z)

Signature of Addressor or person authorised to telegraph in his name.

* This line should be erased if not required.

(632) —McC. & Co. Ltd., London.— W 11400/2045. 100,000 2/15. Forms C 2121/10.

"A" Form. Army Form C. 2121.

MESSAGES AND SIGNALS.

No. of Message

Prefix ..... Code ..... m. Office of Origin and Service Instructions.	Words / Charge	This message is on a/c of: ..... Service. (Signature of "Franking Officer.")	Recd. at ..... m.
2	Sent At ..... m. To ..... By		Date ..... From ..... By .....

TO 23rd Brigade

Sender's Number.	Day of Month	In reply to Number	AAA
* K.O. 4	3/10/15		

The	Germans	are	in	occupation
of	the	WEST	face	of
Redoubt	also	of	a	small
trench	running	south	from	it
in	rear	of	BIG	WILLIE
this	situation	was	far	from
satisfactory	aaa	I	am	digging
tonight	a	trench	running	South
from	my	left	flank	to
face	them	~~aaa~~	but	even
this	will	not	ensure	my
left	flank	with	German	in
South	face	as	well	as
West	face	aaa	The	enemy
is	either	[illegible]	a	force
to	[illegible]	the	Redoubt	in
sufficient	numbers	to	hold	it

From	[illegible]	[illegible] to hold
Place	[illegible] present garrison for a large working	
Time	party under RE supervision to build a fire	

The above may be forwarded as now corrected. ..... Censor.	(Z) ..... Signature of Addressor or person authorised to telegraph in his name.

* This line should be erased if not required.

(632) —McC. & Co. Ltd., London.— W 11400/2045. 100,000. 2/15. Forms C 2121/10.

"A" Form. Army Form C. 2121.

MESSAGES AND SIGNALS.

No. of Message

Prefix ... Code ... m.	Words	Charge	This message is on a/c of:	Recd. at ... m.
Office of Origin and Service Instructions.	Sent		... Service.	Date
	At ... m.			From
	To			
	By		(Signature of "Franking Officer.")	By

TO

Sender's Number.	Day of Month	In reply to Number	AAA
*			

[illegible]	from	my	left	flank
to	your	WEST	FACE	this
should	be	done	at	once
forming	up	with	British	line
aaa	I	have	[illegible]	[illegible]
communication	whatever	it	has	been
with	6th	Brigade	aaa	

[illegible] Capt Adjt

From OC 4/6 O.R.

Place

Time 10.25 pm

The above may be forwarded as now corrected.

(Z)

Censor. Signature of Addressor or person authorised to telegraph in his name.

* This line should be erased if not required.

(2) —McC. & Co. Ltd., London.— W 11400/2045. 100,000. 2/15. Forms C 2121/10.

"C" Form (Quadruplicate). Army Form C. 2123 A

MESSAGES AND SIGNALS. No. of Message

Charges to Pay £ s. d.	Office Stamp. 2HC 3/10/15

Service Instructions.

Handed in at the Priority LHQ Office, at [illegible] m. Received here at 9.52 [illegible] m.

TO 2/ Kings Own R Lgt Thro' 1st Bde

Sender's Number	Day of Month.	In reply to Number.	AAA
BM 638	3rd		

Endeavour to capture point 60 at W end of Big Willie before dawn aaa am attacking Redoubt at Dawn aaa acknowledge

Received 1.11 am

FROM 83 Bde

PLACE

TIME 1.5 pm

GALE & POLDEN, LTD. PRINTERS, ALDERSHOT. (69,017). Wt. 7981—448. 40,000 Pads. 4/13. W.

"A" Form. Army Form C. 2121.

MESSAGES AND SIGNALS.

No. of Message

Prefix .... Code .... m.	Words	Charge	This message is on a/c of:	Recd. at .... m.
Office of Origin and Service Instructions.	Sent		.... Service.	Date
	At .... m.			From
	To			
	By		(Signature of "Franking Officer.")	By

TO 83rd Brigade

Sender's Number.	Day of Month	In reply to Number	AAA
* KD 6	4/10/15		

Your	BM 638	and	BM 642	received
AAA	This	will	be	~~[illegible]~~
done				

From O.C. [illegible]
Place
Time 7.20 am

The above may be forwarded as now corrected.

Censor.

(Z) [illegible signature]

Signature of Addressor or person authorised to telegraph in his name.

* This line should be erased if not required.

(632) —McC. & Co. Ltd., London.— W 11400/2045. 100,000 2/15. Forms C 2121/10.

"A" Form.

Army Form C. 2121.

MESSAGES AND SIGNALS.

No. of Message

Prefix .... Code .... m. | Words | Charge

Office of Origin and Service Instructions.

Sent

At .... m.

To ....

By ....

This message is on a/c of:

.... *Service.*

(Signature of "Franking Officer.")

Recd. at .... m.

Date ....

From ....

By ....

TO

Sender's Number.	Day of Month	In reply to Number	AAA
* KD.7			

'B' Coy will furnish a party of 6 men with 6 shovels + 3 picks immediately behind the last four sandbag men ready to move up to assist if wanted in barricading the junction of Point 60. (as much use as possible should be made of existing Barricade.

The remainder of A Company will stand by ready with covering fire against SOUTH FACE. A Company will be entirely at the disposal of Lieut Ellis.

B Coy & C Coy will stand by.

From OC [illegible]

Place Bn. H.Q.

Time 2 am

The above may be forwarded as now corrected.

.... *Censor.*

(Z)

Signature of Addressor or person authorised to telegraph in his name.

* This line should be erased if not required.

(632) —McC. & Co. Ltd., London.— W 11400/2045. 100,000. 2/15. Forms C 2121/10.

"A" Form. Army Form C. 2121.

MESSAGES AND SIGNALS. No. of Message

Prefix ..... Code ..... m.	Words	Charge	This message is on a/c of:	Recd. at ..... m.
Office of Origin and Service Instructions.	Sent		..... Service.	Date
	At ..... m.			From
	To			By
	By		(Signature of "Franking Officer.")	

TO O.C. A Coy

Sender's Number.	Day of Month	In reply to Number	AAA
* KD.7			

1. 8 Bombers followed by 4 bayonet men followed by 4 sandbag men.
The above to be followed by 8 bombers 4 Bayonet men 4 Sandbag men.
These will assemble on left side of trench looking towards left flank.
On the right of the trench looking towards left flank the remaining 16 bombers will be under Lieut Sommerville disposed so as to form a ladder to pass up bombs.
That end of the trench will be cleared of everybody except the above named.
The New Trench dug tonight will be garrisoned by 15 Rifles under 2nd Lieut O'Brien to act as a support with rifle fire when required.
These 15 men will occupy point ... as soon as the bombers have successfully taken it.
Their action will be guided by the success or non success of the bombers.

From

Place

Time

The above may be forwarded as now corrected. **(Z)**

Censor. Signature of Addressor or person authorised to telegraph in his name.

* This line should be erased if not required.

(632) —McC. & Co. Ltd., London.— W 11400/2045. 100,000. 2/15. Forms C 2121/10.

MESSAGES AND SIGNALS. No. of Message ______

Prefix ______ Code ______ m.	Words	Charge	This message is on a/c of:	Recd. at ______ m.
Office of Origin and Service Instructions.	Sent		______ Service.	Date ______
Priority	At ______ m.			From ______
	To ______		(Signature of "Franking Officer.")	By ______
	By ______			

TO 4   2/Kings Own Regt.

Sender's Number.	Day of Month	In reply to Number	AAA
* B.M.646	4		

Please report by bearer the situation of your battalion and what progress you made yesterday AAA at Pt ~~Hill~~ 60 British troops are reported in western face of REDOUBT AAA Can you verify this statement

From 83 Brigade

Place

Time 7 a.m.

The above may be forwarded as now corrected. (Z) R. C. Follett

Censor.   Signature of Addressor or person authorised to telegraph in his name.

* This line should be erased if not required.

—McC. & Co. Ltd., London.— W 1789/1402. 150,000. 8/15. Forms C 2121/10.

"C" Form (Duplicate). Army Form C. 2123.

MESSAGES AND SIGNALS. No. of Message

Service Instructions.	Charges to Pay. £ s. d.	Office Stamp. GCC 4/10/15

Handed in at 1st Gds Bde Office 7.30A m. Received 7.40A m.

TO 3rd Coldstream

Sender's Number	Day of Month	In reply to Number	AAA
SC 181	4TH		

For Information of 83rd Bde will you ask the Company on your left what the situation is and if they have got SOUTH FACE

FROM 1st Gds Bde
PLACE & TIME 7.30 AM

(25535). M.R.Co.,Ltd. Wt.W1789/1402. 70,000 Pads—6/15. Forms/C.2123.

"A" Form.

Army Form C. 2121.

MESSAGES AND SIGNALS.

No. of Message

Prefix .... Code .... m. | Words | Charge

Office of Origin and Service Instructions.

Sent
At .... m.
To ....
By ....

This message is on a/c of:
.... *Service.*
(Signature of "Franking Officer.")

Recd. at .... m.
Date ....
From ....
By ....

TO 13[illegible] Brigade

Sender's Number.	Day of Month	In reply to Number	AAA
* KO 8	13/10/15	BM 646	

Three	companies	of	my	Battalion
[illegible]	BIG	WILLIE	to	a point
short	of	junction	WEST	FACE
SOUTH	FACE	BIG	WILLIE	AAA
The	Germans	still	hold	SOUTH
FACE	and	I	have	not as yet
got	in	touch	with	any
British	troops	in	WEST	FACE
but	am	endeavouring	to	do
so	AAA	Returning	[illegible]	following
[illegible]	[illegible]	[illegible]	from	about
8 pm	[illegible]	[illegible]	[illegible]	[illegible]
left	[illegible]	[illegible]	[illegible]	[illegible]
SOUTH	FACE	and	DUMP	TRENCH
on	to	the	[illegible]	the
strong	[illegible]	[illegible]	[illegible]	[illegible]
[illegible]	Point	to	[illegible]	[illegible]

From
Place
Time

The above may be forwarded as now corrected. (Z)

.... *Censor.* Signature of Addressor or person authorised to telegraph in his

* This line should be erased if not required.

(632) —McC. & Co. Ltd., London.— W 11400/2045. 100,000. 2/15. Forms C 2121/10.

"A" Form.

Army Form C. 2121.

MESSAGES AND SIGNALS.

No. of Message

Prefix .... Code .... m. | Words | Charge

Office of Origin and Service Instructions.

Sent
At .... m.
To ....
By ....

This message is on a/c of:
.... *Service.*
(Signature of "Franking Officer.")

Recd. at .... m.
Date ....
From ....
By ....

TO { 1 Guards Brigade

Sender's Number.	Day of Month	In reply to Number	AAA
* KO 7	8/10/15	SC 101	

~~[illegible]~~	~~[illegible]~~	~~[illegible]~~	~~[illegible]~~	~~[illegible]~~
Please	inform	83rd	Brigade	enemy
still	in	SOUTH	FACE	enemy have
Bombed	towards	Point	60	without
success	which	they	still	hold

From OC 5th Kings Own

Place

Time 8 20 am

[illegible] Capt Adjt
[illegible]

The above may be forwarded as now corrected.

.... *Censor.*

(Z)

.... Signature of Addressor or person authorised to telegraph in his name.

* This line should be erased if not required.

(632) —McC. & Co. Ltd., London.— W 11400/2045. 100,000. 2/15. Forms C 2121/10.

"A" Form. Army Form C. 2121.

MESSAGES AND SIGNALS.

No. of Message ....

Prefix ..... Code ..... m.	Words	Charge	*This message is on a/c of:*	Recd. at ..... m.
Office of Origin and Service Instructions.	Sent		..... *Service.*	Date .....
	At ..... m.			From .....
	To			By .....
	By		(Signature of "Franking Officer.")	

TO

Sender's Number.	Day of Month	In reply to Number	AAA

*

[illegible] WINDOW AAA [illegible] 5.45 p.m. [illegible]

From [illegible]
Place
Time [illegible]

The above may be forwarded as now corrected.

(Z) [illegible signature]

..... Censor.

Signature of Addressor or person authorised to telegraph in his name.

* This line should be erased if not required.

(632) —McC. & Co. Ltd., London.— W 11400/2045. 100,000. 2/15. Forms C 2121/10.

"A" Form. Army Form C. 2121.

MESSAGES AND SIGNALS.

No. of Message

Prefix .... Code .... m.	Words	Charge	This message is on a/c of:	Recd. at .... m.
Office of Origin and Service Instructions.	Sent		.... Service.	Date ....
5	At .... m.			From ....
	To			
	By		(Signature of "Franking Officer.")	By ....

TO 83 [illegible]

Sender's Number.	Day of Month	In reply to Number	AAA
* KO 19	4/10/15	BM 648	

(A)	Big	[illegible]	[illegible]	[illegible]
[illegible]	[illegible]	[illegible]	can	[illegible]
[illegible]	[illegible]	[illegible]	[illegible]	[illegible]
(B)	[illegible]	[illegible]	SOUTH	FACE
[illegible]	[illegible]	[illegible]	[illegible]	[illegible]
[illegible]	[illegible]	[illegible]	to	[illegible]
[illegible]	a	[illegible]	[illegible]	[illegible]
[illegible]	[illegible]	as	I	[illegible]
[illegible]	[illegible]	[illegible]	Remaining	[illegible]
no	Emplacements	the	[illegible]	[illegible]
[illegible]	[illegible]	as	[illegible]	[illegible]
[illegible]				[illegible]
(C)	Wire	and	Sandbags.	[illegible]
[illegible]	yet	[illegible]	[illegible]	[illegible]
(D) [illegible]	[illegible]	[illegible]	[illegible]	[illegible]
[illegible]	as	for		

From

Place

Time

The above may be forwarded as now corrected. (Z)

Censor. Signature of Addressor or person authorised to telegraph in his name.

* This line should be erased if not required.

(632) —McC. & Co. Ltd., London.— W 11400/2045. 100,000. 2/15. Forms C 2121/10.

MESSAGES AND SIGNALS. No. of Message

Prefix / Code / m.	Words / Charge	This message is on a/c of:	Recd. at m.
Office of Origin and Service Instructions.	Sent At m. To By	Service. (Signature of "Franking Officer.")	Date From By

TO O.C. 2/ Kings Own Regt

Sender's Number.	Day of Month	In reply to Number	AAA
* B.M. 848.	5		

Please send me by bearer the situation regarding your position in BIG WILLIE – Is Big Willie wired on either or both sides? Have you mounted your MGs in it? – The G.O.C. Division is very anxious to know if you could rush Point 60 and work round it by bombing into SOUTH FACE – Any suggestions you have I should like at once – and any offensive movement proposed by you I should like to have details of proposals – It is proposed to dig a C.T. from BIG Willie to British front line – a telephone wire is being laid to you from Bde H.Q. Keep me informed of all that is going on as early as possible –

Send back ~~either~~ the bearer with answer and another man to act as runner.

[illegible] Ravenshaw
Brig. Genl.
83rd Inf. Bde

From
Place
Time 1 pm

The above may be forwarded as now corrected. (Z)

Censor. Signature of Addressor or person authorised to telegraph in his name.

* This line should be erased if not required.

(774-5) —McC. & Co. Ltd., London.— W 1739/1402. 150,000. 8/15. Forms C 2121/10.

"A" Form.

Army Form C. 2121.

MESSAGES AND SIGNALS.

No. of Message

Prefix ______ Code ______ m.	Words	Charge	This message is on a/c of:	Recd. at ______ m.
Office of Origin and Service Instructions.	Sent		______ Service.	Date
	At ______ m.			From
	To			By
	By		(Signature of "Franking Officer.")	

TO

Sender's Number.	Day of Month	In reply to Number	AAA
*			

[illegible]	[illegible]	[illegible]	[illegible]	[illegible]
[illegible]	[illegible]	[illegible]	[illegible]	[illegible]
[illegible]	[illegible]	[illegible]	[illegible]	[illegible]
[illegible]	[illegible]	[illegible]	[illegible]	[illegible]
[illegible]	[illegible]	[illegible]	[illegible]	[illegible]
[illegible]	[illegible]	[illegible]	offensive	[illegible]
[illegible]	[illegible]	present	position	[illegible]
[illegible]	[illegible]	[illegible]	[illegible]	[illegible]
[illegible]	[illegible]	[illegible]	[illegible]	[illegible]
[illegible]	[illegible]	[illegible]	[illegible]	[illegible]
[illegible]	[illegible]	[illegible]	[illegible]	[illegible]
[illegible]	[illegible]	(b) Point	[illegible]	[illegible]
[illegible]	position	[illegible]	[illegible]	[illegible]
[illegible]	approach	for	[illegible]	[illegible]
[illegible]	[illegible]	am	only	able
[illegible]	hold	any	present	[illegible]
[illegible]	[illegible]	[illegible]	[illegible]	being

From

Place

Time

The above may be forwarded as now corrected.

Censor.

(Z)

Signature of Addressor or person authorised to telegraph in his name.

* This line should be erased if not required.

(632) —McC. & Co. Ltd., London.— W 11400/2045. 100,000 2/15. Forms C 2121/10.

"A" Form. Army Form C. 2121.

MESSAGES AND SIGNALS.

No. of Message

Prefix .... Code .... m.	Words	Charge	This message is on a/c of:	Recd. at .... m.
Office of Origin and Service Instructions.	Sent		.... Service.	Date
	At .... m.			From
	To			By
	By		(Signature of "Franking Officer.")	

TO

Sender's Number.	Day of Month	In reply to Number	AAA
*			

[illegible]	[illegible]	enemy	[illegible]	[illegible]
[illegible]	[illegible]	[illegible]	[illegible]	[illegible]
[illegible]	[illegible]	[illegible]	[illegible]	[illegible]
[illegible]	[illegible]	[illegible]	[illegible]	[illegible]
[illegible]	[illegible]	[illegible]	[illegible]	[illegible]
[illegible]	that	[illegible]	[illegible]	movement
[illegible]	my	present	position	[illegible]
[illegible]	[illegible]	on	[illegible]	[illegible]
[illegible]	[illegible]	[illegible]	[illegible]	[illegible]
[illegible]	[illegible]	[illegible]	[illegible]	[illegible]
[illegible]	[illegible]	[illegible]	[illegible]	[illegible]
[illegible]	[illegible]	(6) Point	[illegible]	[illegible]
[illegible]	position	[illegible]	three	[illegible]
[illegible]	[illegible]	[illegible]	enemy	[illegible]
[illegible]	I	am	only	able
to	hold	my	present	position
[illegible]	[illegible]	[illegible]	[illegible]	[illegible]

From			
Place			
Time			

The above may be forwarded as now corrected. (Z)

Censor. Signature of Addressor or person authorised to telegraph in his name.

* This line should be erased if not required.

(632) —McC. & Co. Ltd., London.— W 11400/2045. 100,000. 2/15. Forms C 2121/10.

MESSAGES AND SIGNALS. No. of Message

Prefix .... Code .... m. | Words | Charge | This message is on a/c of: .... Service. (Signature of "Franking Officer.") | Recd. at .... m. Date .... From .... By ....

Office of Origin and Service Instructions. Sent At .... m. To .... By ....

TO: O.C. 2/ Kings Own Regt

Sender's Number.	Day of Month	In reply to Number	
* B.M. 648.	5		AAA

Please send me by bearer the situation regarding your position in BIG WILLIE – Is Big Willie wired on either or both sides? Have you mounted your MGs in it? – The 28th Division is very anxious to know if you could rush point 60 and work round it by bombing the SOUTH FACE – Any suggestions you have I should like at once – and any offensive movement possible by you I should like to have details of the operation – It is proposed to dig a C.T. from BIG Willie to British front line – a telephone wire is being laid to you from Bde H.Q. Keep me informed of all that is going on as early as possible –

Send back ~~either~~ the bearer with answers and another orderly to act as runner.

H. S. L. Ravenshaw
Bt Genl
83rd Inf. Bde

From Bde
Place
Time 1 pm

The above may be forwarded as now corrected. (Z)

Censor. Signature of Addressor or person authorised to telegraph in his name.

* This line should be erased if not required.

(774-5) —McC. & Co. Ltd., London.— W 1789/1462. 150,000. 8/15. Forms C 2121/10.

"A" Form. Army Form C. 2121.

MESSAGES AND SIGNALS.

No. of Message

Prefix ______ Code ______ m.	Words	Charge	This message is on a/c of:	Recd. at ______ m.
Office of Origin and Service Instructions.	Sent		______ Service.	Date
5	At ______ m.			From
	To			By
	By		(Signature of "Franking Officer.")	

TO 83 Brigade

Sender's Number.	Day of Month	In reply to Number	AAA
* VO 12	4/16/15	B.M. 648	

(A) Big [illegible] will [illegible] I [illegible] [illegible] [illegible] [illegible] [illegible] [illegible] [illegible] [illegible] [illegible] [illegible] (B) [illegible] [illegible] [illegible] [illegible] [illegible] [illegible] [illegible] [illegible] [illegible] [illegible] [illegible] fire [illegible] enfilade [illegible] a position to [illegible] on [illegible] They are I have [illegible] [illegible] as [illegible] Remaining [illegible] no emplacements the [illegible] wrong [illegible] [illegible] as [illegible] [illegible] (C) Wire and Sandbags have [illegible] yet finished [illegible] [illegible] [illegible] [illegible] if [illegible] [illegible] (D) [illegible] [illegible] [illegible] for [illegible] [illegible] [illegible] as

From

Place

Time

The above may be forwarded as now corrected. (Z)

Censor. Signature of Addressor or person authorised to telegraph in his name.

* This line should be erased if not required.

(632) —McC. & Co. Ltd., London.— W 11400/2045. 100,000. 2/15. Forms C 2121/10.

"A" Form.

Army Form C. 2121.

MESSAGES AND SIGNALS.

No. of Message ....

Prefix ..... Code ..... m.	Words	Charge	*This message is on a/c of:*	Recd. at ..... m.
Office of Origin and Service Instructions.	Sent		..... *Service.*	Date .....
	At ..... m.			From .....
	To		(Signature of "Franking Officer.")	By .....
	By			

TO

Sender's Number.	Day of Month	In reply to Number	A A A
*			

[illegible]

From [illegible]

Place [illegible]

Time 3.10 am

The above may be forwarded as now corrected.

(Z)

..... *Censor.*

Signature of Addressor or person authorised to telegraph in his name.

* This line should be erased if not required.

(632) —McC. & Co. Ltd., London.— W 11400/2045. 100,000. 2/15. Forms C 2121/10.

"A" Form.

Army Form C

MESSAGES AND SIGNALS.

No. of Message

Prefix .... Code .... m.	Words	Charge	This message is on a/c of:	Recd. at ....
Office of Origin and Service Instructions.	Sent		.... Service.	Date ....
	At .... m.			From ....
	To			
	By		(Signature of "Franking Officer.")	By ....

TO

Sender's Number.	Day of Month	In reply to Number	AAA
*			

From

Place

Time

The above may be forwarded as now corrected.

(Z)

Censor.

Signature of Addressor or person authorised to telegraph in his name.

* This line should be erased if not required.

(632) —McC. & Co. Ltd., London.— W 11400/2045. 100,000. 2/15. Forms C 2121/10.

"A" Form.

Army Form C. 2121.

MESSAGES AND SIGNALS.

No. of Message

Prefix .... Code .... m.	Words	Charge	This message is on a/c of:	Recd. at .... m.
Office of Origin and Service Instructions.	Sent		.... Service.	Date
	At .... m.			From
	To			By
	By		(Signature of "Franking Officer.")	

TO

Sender's Number.	Day of Month	In reply to Number	AAA
*			

[illegible]	[illegible]	troops	having	[illegible]
[illegible]	a	[illegible]	[illegible]	[illegible]
[illegible]	through	[illegible]	[illegible]	[illegible]
[illegible]	[illegible]	~~[illegible]~~	~~[illegible]~~	~~[illegible]~~
[illegible]	[illegible]	[illegible]	[illegible]	[illegible]
[illegible]	[illegible]	[illegible]	especially	[illegible]
[illegible]	[illegible]			

[illegible signature]

From [illegible]

Place [illegible]

Time 3.15 pm

The above may be forwarded as now corrected.

Censor.

(Z) Signature of Addressor or person authorised to telegraph in his name.

* This line should be erased if not required.

C. & Co. Ltd., London.— W 11400/2045. 100,000. 2/15. Forms C 2121/10.

"A" Form. Army Form C. 2121.

MESSAGES AND SIGNALS.

No. of Message

Prefix ...... Code ...... m. | Words | Charge

Office of Origin and Service Instructions.

6

Sent
At ...... m.
To ......
By ......

This message is on a/c of: ...... Service.

(Signature of "Franking Officer.")

Recd. at ...... m.
Date ......
From ......
By ......

TO 15th Brigade.

Sender's Number.	Day of Month	In reply to Number	AAA
* RS 21	3/10/15		

[illegible] 2 am [illegible]

From [illegible]
Place [illegible]
Time 8.32 am

The above may be forwarded as now corrected.

Censor.

(Z)

Signature of Addressor or person authorised to telegraph in his name.

* This line should be erased if not required.

(632) —McC. & Co. Ltd., London.— W 11400/2045. 100,000. 2/15. Forms C 2121/10.

"A" Form. Army Form C. 2121.

MESSAGES AND SIGNALS.

No. of Message

Prefix .... Code .... m.	Words	Charge	*This message is on a/c of:*	Recd. at .... m.
Office of Origin and Service Instructions.	Sent		.... *Service.*	Date ....
	At .... m.			From ....
	To			
	By		(Signature of "Franking Officer.")	By ....

TO

Sender's Number.	Day of Month	In reply to Number	A A A
*			

From

Place

Time

The above may be forwarded as now corrected.

Censor.

(Z)

Signature of Addressor or person authorised to telegraph in his name.

* This line should be erased if not required.

(632) —McC. & Co. Ltd., London.— W 11400/2045. 100,000. 2/15. Forms C 2121/10.

www.ingramcontent.com/pod-product-compliance
Lightning Source LLC
Chambersburg PA
CBHW081431160426
43193CB00013B/2251